GREATEST GAMES
SHEFFIELD UNITED

GREATEST GAMES
SHEFFIELD UNITED

BLADES' FIFTY
FINEST MATCHES

MATT ANSON

First published by Pitch Publishing, 2019

Pitch Publishing
A2 Yeoman Gate
Yeoman Way
Worthing
Sussex
BN13 3QZ
www.pitchpublishing.co.uk
info@pitchpublishing.co.uk

A CIP catalogue record is available for this book
from the British Library.

ISBN 978 1 78531 550 3

Typesetting and origination by Pitch Publishing
Printed and bound in India by Replika Press Pvt. Ltd.

Contents

Dedication

To my wife, Derve, for constant
belief and encouragement, and our
wonderful kids Amy & Harry.
UTB
x

Acknowledgements

While this book was a lot of fun to write, there were times when hunting down specific information, or match reports of any real use, became an arduous task. There are a number of people, publications and organisations that I couldn't have done this without, even if it was just for pointing me in the right direction in some cases.

Starting with the people I had direct contact with during the writing of the book: Firstly, the fellow Blades fans – Robin Wiltshire at Sheffield Archives (www.sheffield.gov.uk/archives) who was a huge help, as was Phil Parker, who dug out his scrapbook for match reports on 1970s and 80s games. Also, John Garrett, SUFC Club Engagement Manager, Christian Nade for the impromptu interview over LinkedIn and everyone at the #WeAreUnited Facebook group who provided me with their lists of favourite games. Thanks too to Gareth Davis, co-author of *Greatest Games: Derby County* for the early advice and Rob Grillo, a Bradford Park Avenue fan who was able to provide me with a piece of missing information.

Writing a book like this is a lot easier when much groundwork has been laid, and the work that Denis Clarebrough and Andrew Kirkham have done over the years is immense, as is the work that must go into setting up and maintaining the English National Football Archive (www.enfa.co.uk) and the British Newspaper Archive (https://www.britishnewspaperarchive.co.uk/).

Thanks also to Paul and Jane Camillin and Duncan Olner at Pitch Publishing for making this all possible.

Finally, this book would never have happened had my parents not brought me up as a Blades fan, so thanks to them, and also to Andy Mills for the many lifts to away games and ticket dig-outs over the years, especially QPR after I'd had a curry the night before, and getting him lost in Stockport.

Introduction

This book began as another idea, namely, to choose the best game of each season of United's history, but Paul at Pitch Publishing didn't think the idea would work. In fairness, he was right. How do you pick a highlight from 1980/81 or 2010/11, for instance?

Paul pointed me in the direction of the 'Greatest Games' series, which is a much better format than the one I had in mind, so then it was a matter of selecting the games. One difficulty was that the heyday of both Sheffield clubs was before the Second World War. They won 12 major trophies between them before 1939, one since (and that was just a League Cup), and United's golden period was at the turn of the last century, and this was also part of a 41-year unbroken spell in the top flight. It would be wrong not to include the trophy wins, and some key matches from that era, and I know I found a lot of the stories fascinating. I hope I conveyed them well here, and that readers find the balance right between nostalgia and history.

League championships and FA Cups apart, success is relative. To help me pick the more recent games, I posted on a large Blades social media group to list their favourites and Darlington away in the Fourth Division was a consistent choice with Blades of a certain age. Many neutrals may also be surprised at the inclusion of a defeat, against Hull in the 2014 FA Cup semi, but, again, context is everything and the goals and performance in that game meant so much to Blades fans.

I was also pleased that the 6-3 win against Orient in 1984 kept coming up on people's lists, as I had procrastinated on its inclusion in case it was just a case of self-indulgence, as I was fortunate enough that this was my first Blades match.

Probably the biggest internal debate I had was around the 2002/03 season, which is represented by four games here, when no other season had more than two games included. It was an incredible season, but that is tempered by the fact that it finished empty-handed, but which game of the four included here could I leave out?

Of course, being a book about Sheffield United, our neighbours from South Barnsley (sorry, Sheffield 6) loom large, and nine of the games are against our city rivals. I questioned whether to include each one, not least to avoid any accusation of the Blades support being 'obsessed' by them. But both Sheffield clubs ARE defined by the other, like it or not. Your city rivals are your yardstick for success, and the balance of power in Sheffield has shifted so many times, that it is impossible not to measure yourself against the other team. Any Wednesdayite (or Blade for that matter) who says they do not is not being honest with you or themselves, and deep down we're all thankful that we are a two-club city and not, say, Leeds, as being able to put one over our friends, colleagues and family who support the other lot adds that bit more spice to matchdays.

I have to say the process of writing this book has been hugely enjoyable, if at times a bit of a slog (the completist in me just had to know who managed Bradford PA in 1946, that one-line gap in the book would have haunted me forever), and I hope it is both informative as well as bringing back great memories, and reminds us all why we are Blades in the first place.

Matt Anson, March 2019
mattanson1889@gmail.com

v The Wednesday 3-2

Friendly Match
12 January 1891
Bramall Lane
Attendance: 14,000

SHEFFIELD UNITED	THE WEDNESDAY
Howlett	Smith
Whitham	Thompson
Lilley	Brayshaw
Cross	Brandon, H.
Howell	Ingram
Groves	Cawley
Shaw	Winterbottom
Bridgewater	Mumford
Robertson	Brandon, R.
Watson	Woolhouse
Calder	Hodder
Secretary: J.B. Wolstenholm	Club Captain: Haydn Morley

If a Sheffielder responds to a question of where they are from, more often than not the next question will be 'United or Wednesday?' This happens to people from the city wherever they travel in the world. It is hard to imagine a time in Sheffield without the two clubs, but people have lived in or around the area for 12 millennia, and the existence of the two clubs is a small fraction of this time. But football is part of the city's DNA now, arguably these days more synonymous with Sheffield than steel or cutlery.

The city that is the home of the world's oldest club (1857) also boasts a number of other football firsts: the first codified rules of football (1858); the first game between two clubs (1860) which is also the oldest local derby (Sheffield against Hallam); the first cup competition, the Youdan Cup (1867); the first floodlit game (1878), which was played at Bramall Lane.

In 1867, The Wednesday Cricket Club decided to form a football offshoot, playing at Bramall Lane. After moving to professional status, the club decided they would be unable to continue paying their landlords and would need to develop their own ground, eventually moving just down the road to Olive Grove in 1887.

The loss of rental income from Wednesday led to discussions by the Bramall Lane committee, led by Charles Clegg, of forming their own club. On 16 March 1889, the stadium held the FA Cup semi-final between 'The Invincibles', Preston, and West Brom, attracting a huge crowd of 22,688. This was the catalyst that Clegg needed and six days later the club was founded.

By August they were playing their first official game, a 4-1 reversal at Notts Rangers with a side containing a mixture of local players and Scottish professionals. Although United's first signings would prove inadequate, two of them would have an impact on the club's early history. Charlie Howlett was their first goalkeeper, and he continued to play while United rose to the top flight of the Football League, while forward W. Robertson, one of the Scottish professionals, had the unique combined honour of scoring United's first-ever goal, first hat-trick, and first FA Cup goal.

As United found their feet, Wednesday had become members of the Football Alliance, winning it at the first attempt and also reaching the FA Cup Final, losing 6-1 to Blackburn Rovers in 1890.

United, perhaps understandably given that Wednesday were playing a higher quality of opposition, were charging half the price for tickets compared to Wednesday, but the older club saw this as an attempt to undercut them. United, meanwhile, felt that Wednesday were using more than their fair share of free Saturdays. They had also attempted to sign four Wednesday players in the summer of 1890, including future United trainer George Waller, only thwarted by incorrect paperwork! This was a fight for the supremacy of the city, perhaps even for survival, and the Sheffield public were desperate to see a meeting of the two clubs. Two 'friendly' games were arranged for the 1890/91 season, the first at Olive Grove in December, with the reverse fixture the following month.

After 20 minutes of the Olive Grove fixture, Robertson added to his already impressive list of 'firsts' by scoring the first-ever goal in a Sheffield derby. Despite this opener, Wednesday scored two second-half goals in fading light to win the game, although the local press felt that United deserved to draw the game.

This had taken place in what was known locally as the Calf, Cow and Bull weeks, when local workers allowed themselves no time off work to save up for Christmas, but the game was so eagerly anticipated that, even with kick-off at 2.30pm on a Monday, it proved too strong to resist for 10,000 supporters, undeterred by some really miserable weather. United had undergone squad strengthening during the year, having joined the Midland League, and only Robertson and Howlett had survived from the first-ever game. Perhaps the most notable of the signings were midfielder Rab Howell and defender Mick Whitham, both signed from Rotherham Swifts, and full-back Harry Lilley from Staveley.

Lilley and Whitham would become, in 1892, the first United players to be selected for England. Howell came from a local gypsy family, and he would feature for United for the next eight years, winning two England caps.

With first blood going to Wednesday at Olive Grove, and neither team making any progress in their leagues, the return fixture was the main attraction for Sheffield football fans in the second half of the season. Would Wednesday do the double, or would United gain revenge and make it 'honours even'?

Such was the interest that house windows and telegraph poles surrounding Bramall Lane were utilised by those unable to gain entry to the packed ground. The reported attendance was 14,000, which was to this point the largest crowd to attend a Sheffield club game.

An even first half finished goalless, but wasn't without incident, including the inevitable dog on the pitch and a mini pitch invasion from supporters at the Shoreham Street end. Wednesday, however, took the lead after 61 minutes. Ingram, who had swapped positions with Mumford at half-time, scored the goal with a fast, low shot. Three minutes later, it was 2-0 to the team in blue and white, Cawley's free kick put home by Bob Brandon. The double, and Sheffield supremacy, was in Wednesday's hands.

The game opened up, and another goal came just six minutes later. United won a corner, which George Groves played to Arthur Watson, who shot quickly to pull a goal back. This electrified United, who began to cause Wednesday problems with attack after attack until a high shot by Howell beat Smith in the Wednesday goal to level the scores. Both teams dug deep into their reserves of stamina.

With five minutes remaining, United won the ball in midfield and Bridgewater played a through-ball to Calder, who hit the ball sweetly to put United in the lead for the first time. Wednesday defenders appealed for an offside decision. It was close, according to contemporary accounts, but the goal was awarded by the officials.

'This led,' wrote the *Sheffield Independent*, 'to a throwing up of hats and a very peculiar sort of joyful exclamation – I am unable to spell the sound.'

United held on, and, as the full-time whistle sounded, the spectators swarmed on to the pitch to cheer off both teams. Over the two games, honours were even, but United had, not for the last time, come back from two goals behind in a derby game.

United applied to join the Football Alliance the following season but were rejected on the grounds that they didn't want multiple teams from the same city. This argument was weak considering that they already had both Birmingham St George's and Small Heath in the league, and at the same time as rejecting United, had agreed to admit Ardwick (the future Manchester City) – despite Newton Heath (the future Manchester United) already being members.

United felt that Wednesday had a hand in the rejection, although they firmly denied this, but bad feeling between the two teams continued to grow. The next season, they faced one another again in 'friendly' games, United triumphed 5-0 at Bramall Lane but lost 4-1 at Olive Grove, and there were reports of fighting amongst supporters. By 1893, the two teams were facing each in league football at last, in the First Division of the Football League. The first game at Bramall Lane ended in a 1-1 draw in front of, to that point, a Sheffield record 27,000 crowd, while United won 2-1 at Olive Grove.

Football has changed hugely since those early days, but, still, no fixture is so eagerly anticipated, or dreaded, by Sheffield football fans as when the two teams face one another. If the teams are in the same division, they will always be the first dates looked for when the fixture list is published. In this aspect, nothing has changed in over a century.

v Burslem Port Vale 10-0

Football League Second Division
10 December 1892
Cobridge Athletic Ground, Stoke-on-Trent
Attendance: 1,500

SHEFFIELD UNITED	BURSLEM PORT VALE
Howlett	Farrington
Whitham	Clutton
Lilley	McAlpine
Howell	Delve
Hendry	McCrindle
Needham	Ditchfield
Drummond	Garner
Wallace	Mountford
Hammond	Beech
Davies	Bliss
Watson	Scarrett
Secretary: J.B. Wolstenholm	Club Captain: Enoch Hood

The Football League was launched in 1889, and, after some initial success, a decision was made to add a second 'division' of 14 clubs. Promotion and relegation between the two was to be decided by 'Test' matches of the top three versus the bottom three in the First Division. United were elected to the new Second Division while Wednesday were one of the two expansion teams for the First Division, which added to the bad feeling that already existed between the two clubs.

United opened their life in the Football League with a 4-2 win over Lincoln City, Harry Hammond scoring United's first league goal on his way to a hat-trick. Signed from Everton in 1891, he would also become the first United player to be sent off in a league match, away at Crewe.

The Blades boasted a 100 percent home record until early January, dropping just one point at home all season. Their initial away form, though, was poor. The first point of the season away from Bramall Lane had been picked up at Small Heath (later Birmingham City) the week prior to the meeting with Burslem Port Vale. Vale had, however, suffered a few heavy defeats already, most recently a 5-0 hammering at Crewe on 26 November. On the same day, United had destroyed Bootle 8-3 at Bramall Lane. Despite these results, nobody could possibly have predicted the events of Sheffield United's trip to Staffordshire.

United were led on to the field by Billy Hendry, who had established himself as an extremely effective captain since joining from Preston the previous season. He brought a high level of both leadership and tactical nous, as well as a good level of playing ability. He was also influential in the development of Ernest Needham, who would succeed him as captain and would lead United to the club's greatest successes. Also joining from Preston with Hendry was forward Jack Drummond.

At Burslem's ground in Cobridge, the pitch was covered with at least three inches of snow, which continued to fall throughout the game. Vale were missing their regular goalkeeper and two key players. 'From the start the home club were no match for their rivals,' wrote *The Sportsman*. United employed a short, quick passing game to counteract the windy conditions and took just two minutes to open the scoring through Drummond with a swift, low effort. In the third minute, Sandy Wallace latched on to an Arthur Watson through-ball and gave Farrington in the Vale goal no chance. Next, Hendry broke up a Burslem attack, fed Drummond on the right to bring the ball forward and pass to Hammond, who dribbled past two defending players before firing home. The Vale keeper was called into action twice more in the next few minutes, then clever passing play between Fred Davies and Watson fooled the defence, Watson unleashing a powerful shot into the net. Eleven minutes gone, 4-0.

The United halves and backs found winning the ball easy, and the United goalkeeper Charlie Howlett didn't touch the ball until the 25th minute, although one Vale effort had cleared the bar a moment earlier.

Drummond's long dribbles down the right caused Vale problems, and he linked up with Hammond again in the 28th minute. This time, Hammond fed Watson this time, who fired home.

Early in the second half, United keeper Howlett was called into action at last, and he made a good save. Drummond then headed in United's sixth, Watson this time the provider. After 61 minutes, Davies ran through the defence with the ball and finished well and it took him just another minute to register his second and the Blades' eighth, again Drummond key in the build-up.

The United forwards took a well-earned breather now, their fast play on the heavy snow catching up with them and the backs – Mick Whitham, Ernest Needham and Rab Howell – took on the hard work for a while. Howlett, too, was called into action to make a fine save when Burslem looked certain to score.

A former Vale player in the crowd, having had a few too many drinks to beat the cold, decided he could do a better job than the current crop and took it upon himself to take the field, causing a slight delay before he was abruptly removed and dumped in a bank of snow by Billy Hendry. This seemed to have given the United forwards the chance to regain their energy. Good interplay between the forward line tee up Hammond to complete his hat-trick. This was his second hat-trick in two weeks, after scoring five in the Bootle game.

The crowd called for double figures, and the team granted their wish in the 80th minute, following tricky play by Hammond before he fired home.

This was only the third time a team had scored double figures in the Football League and to this day remains the only time by an away team to do so.

The return fixture was played the following week at Bramall Lane, United winning 4-0 with Hammond and Drummond again on the scoresheet. Hammond would finish as the team's top scorer in the league, with 18 goals in as many games, and would be a regular in the Blades' line-up for another five years before joining Leicester, for whom he scored their first league goal just as he had done for the Blades.

United did not lose another Football League game all season, which resulted in a second-place finish and a 'Test' match against Accrington who had finished in the bottom three of the First Division. United won 1-0, Drummond scoring the only goal of the game. United had won promotion to the First Division at the first attempt. They would remain there for 41 years.

v Bolton Wanderers 1-0
Football League First Division
8 April 1898
Burnden Park, Bolton
Attendance: 19,395

SHEFFIELD UNITED	BOLTON WANDERERS
Foulke	Sutcliffe
Thickett	Somerville
Cain	Jones
Johnson	Fitchett
Morren	Brown
Howard	Freebairn
Bennett	Thompson
Needham	Gilligan
Almond	Cassidy
Cunningham	Nicol
Priest	Gregory
Secretary: J.B. Wolstenholm	Manager: Frank Brettell

The two most common answers when the question is asked, 'Who is Sheffield United's greatest-ever player?' are Jimmy Hagan and Tony Currie. When the club celebrated 125 years in 2014, a public poll selected Currie.

Of course, the answer is purely subjective, and in 100 years from now, possibly a player from the 21st century will be the answer given, Hagan and Currie remembered only in history books and, in Currie's case, grainy colour TV footage.

Based on achievements in the game for club and country, though, both Hagan and Currie fall short of another past player. That man is Ernest Needham. To this day, he is the only Sheffield United player to captain England, and he earned twice as many England caps (16) as any other Blades player, and double that of Currie and Hagan's totals combined.

He is the only Sheffield United captain to lift the Football League championship trophy with the club. He was also the captain for the only two seasons where the club finished as runners-up. He lifted the FA Cup twice, and was also a beaten finalist once.

In fact, not only could Needham lay claim to being United's best player, in his own time there were those who claimed he was the best player in England and, therefore, as the game was still to become truly international, the best in the world. So respected was Needham in the game, that he was able to publish a critically acclaimed book on the game while still a player.

Signed from Staveley in 1891, Needham started as a right-sided forward for United before being moved back to the half-back line (the equivalent of a defensive midfielder today), where he stayed for almost two decades. On 7 April 1894, Needham made his debut for England in a 2-2 draw at Celtic Park against Scotland. In his absence, United lost their first league game since January.

By 1895, the 'midget' half-back line of Rab Howell, Tommy Morren and Needham was a key part of the United style of play, winning the ball and playing long passes to the wings while also contributing to a formidable defence, backed by legendary keeper William Foulke. At 5ft 5in tall, Needham was a strong stocky but also fast and seemingly able to run forever, contributing to both defence and attack and leading him to be nicknamed 'the Prince of half-backs'. Indeed, the question could be asked, why is there no statue of Ernest Needham outside Bramall Lane alongside Joe Shaw and Derek Dooley?

On Good Friday 1898, he led out a United team at Burnden Park within a whisker of winning a first Football League championship. They had lost just two games before February, including two wins on consecutive Saturdays against reigning champions Villa, effectively knocking them out of the title race. The second game, at Villa, was played in front of a then league record of 43,000 spectators. In his book, *Association Football,* Needham listed the game as one of the great games in which he'd played. 'Luck seemed against us early in the game,' he wrote, 'and we soon lost the services of our centre-forward [Ralph Gaudie], who retired with a broken nose. He did not return until ten minutes from the finish, and then the Villans were leading by one to none. But this was Cunningham's day, and he showed it by scoring two goals in the last three minutes. What a sensational finish!'

Following this, a shock FA Cup defeat to Burslem Port Vale preceded a dip in form, allowing Sunderland, now in second place, to narrow the gap. United travelled to the Wearsiders' ground at Newcastle Road and lost 3-1, thanks largely to two bizarre own goals from Rab Howell. Although no official allegations of match-fixing were brought against Howell, his eight-year tenure as a United player was brought swiftly to an end, and he was transferred to Liverpool after one last appearance for the Blades.

United gained revenge for the defeat by beating Sunderland at Bramall Lane the following Saturday and, by the time they travelled to relegation-strugglers Bolton on Good Friday, they were three points clear with two games remaining. A win, and Sunderland failing to win at Bury, would seal the league championship for the Blades.

Great Central Railways had laid on a train from Sheffield Victoria station, and hundreds of Unitedites had made the journey to cheer the side on, on a glorious, sunny day. The attendance was a new record for Bolton Wanderers,

United made a few changes to recent line-ups. Needham moved into the forward line in place of the absent George Hedley, with Harry Howard taking his place at half-back.

Despite a bright start from Bolton, United soon took control of the game with accurate passing and good play on the wings, Jack Almond shooting just wide and Needham putting over the bar from a cross by Walter 'Cocky' Bennett. Bolton's Cassidy did, however, put a shot about a foot wide of Foulke's goal. Fred Priest picked up an injury in a scramble in the Bolton goalmouth, simultaneously spraining both knee and ankle, and was effectively a passenger for the rest of the game. 'Had he been in his usual condition there is little or no doubt but that he would have scored at least two goals, if not three,' wrote the *Sheffield Independent*.

Captain Needham seemed to cover every inch of the field, and it was fitting that it was he who put United ahead, after 25 minutes, cutting in from the left wing and dribbling past two Bolton defenders to slot past Sutcliffe, falling over the keeper as he followed through his run.

The goal spurred Bolton into life, but Bob Cain and Harry Thickett coped admirably, Harry Johnson cleared one good chance and Foulke fisted clear anything which came in his direction. Needham then again beat the defence and tried to create a replica of the first goal, but Bolton defender Somerville was able to challenge him just as United's inspirational captain was about to shoot.

United had a lucky escape shortly before half-time. Foulke was forced to put the ball behind, and it stopped dead as it just crossed the line. The referee hadn't spotted it going over, and play continued with Foulke stranded, but Bolton failed to take advantage.

Bolton's former Wednesday player, Brown, was forced to retire after a few minutes of the second half as the oppressive heat took its toll, both teams' tiring legs resulting in a drab second half. The Lancastrians were perhaps unlucky not to score in the second half, a good chance wasted high over the bar, while Foulke pulled off a couple of good saves. A wonderful shot from Needham was tipped over the bar by Sutcliffe towards the end of the game. The subsequent corner resulted in a clearance and the referee, Mr West of Lincoln, blew his whistle.

The game had finished 1-0 to United, and news was eagerly awaited of the game a few miles away at Gigg Lane. Billy Barbour had given Bury the lead in the seventh minute, and by half-time, Sunderland had been reduced to nine men through injuries. Bury got the victory, and United were champions. The day after the Bolton game, Foulke, Thickett, Morren and Needham played for the Football League XI against the Scottish League XI at Villa Park. All four would play again for United on Easter Monday, making it three games in four days, as United celebrated their championship with a 2-0 win at home to West Brom. The following Saturday, the Blades would also become 'Champions of Britain' after winning a two-legged tie against Celtic, 2-1 on aggregate. No complaints in those days about congested fixture lists!

We now know that 1897/98 was to be United's only championship win, although they would come close and would also feature strongly in the FA Cup over the next few years. This was, without a doubt, United's golden period, and the man who led them throughout was, of course, Ernest 'Nudger' Needham, the prince of half-backs and the king of Bramall Lane. Surely a statue or a stand named after this legendary player is not asking too much?

v Liverpool 4-4

FA Cup Semi-Final Replay
23 March 1899
Burnden Park, Bolton
Attendance: 20,000

SHEFFIELD UNITED	LIVERPOOL
Foulke	Storer
Thickett	Goldie, A.
Boyle	Dunlop
Johnson	Howell
Morren	Raisbeck
Needham	Goldie, W.
Bennett	Cox
Beer	Walker
Hedley	Allan
Almond	Morgan
Priest	Robertson
Secretary: John Nicholson	Manager: Tom Watson

Just over a year after winning the league title at Burnden Park, United returned to the scene of the triumph for what turned out to be one of the most thrilling cup ties in their history. The team had started its defence of the title strongly, going unbeaten for the first 11 games until losing away at Liverpool. Cain and Howell had moved on, though, and the defence was less tight than it had been in the prior two seasons. There were also a number of injuries to key players, only two games were won away from Bramall Lane, and any ambitions of retaining the trophy were over by New Year.

In the FA Cup, however, the team showed character, and a genuine belief that they could win the trophy for the first time.

In the first round, they were drawn away at Burnley, who had won the Second Division title the previous season and were now challenging to win the First Division. United brought a strong following to Turf Moor, and most observers felt that United deserved to have progressed without the need for a replay. They led twice in the game, a goal by George Hedley was mysteriously disallowed and Burnley's second equaliser was a clear handball into the goal. Tommy Morren scored directly from a free kick in the second half of the replay to win the tie.

The reward was another away trip to top-flight opposition across the Pennines, this time against Preston North End. United trained in Lytham, as they had done for the Burnley game, and, as in that match, drew 2-2. The Blades were dominant in the replay. Preston keeper McBride performed heroics, Needham missed a first-half penalty, but scored one in the second half, which was enough to put United in the quarter-finals for the first time in their history.

The reward was another away tie at a First Division team, and this time it was against the holders, Nottingham Forest. This was United's first trip to the new City Ground and a huge 9,000 Sheffielders made the short trip. By half-time, the Blades were down to ten men due to an injury to Jack Almond, and Needham was a virtual passenger due to being on the receiving end of rough treatment. Showing the character that Needham would later say made him feel like this was their year in the cup, they ground out the result, Foulke pulling off an incredible save before Fred Priest turned home Beer's cross in the 86th minute to send them into the semi-finals.

The draw would pit them against Liverpool, who were top of the league when the teams met. The City Ground was chosen as the neutral venue for the game, and this would be United's third trip to the ground in four games. As before, they took a large support with them.

Hedley scored a tenth-minute opener for the Blades, but five minutes later, George Allan equalised for Liverpool. Allan was well-known to United. Prior to the league meeting at Anfield in October, Allan had claimed that he would knock over the giant Foulke in the Blades' goal. In the game, he attempted to do so, the two players got in a tangle, and the referee gave a penalty which won the game for Liverpool. Another familiar face in the Liverpool line-up was Rab Howell, who had left United the previous year following either a match-fixing or a sex scandal, depending who you listened to at the time!

Allan's goal was added to by Morgan before half-time, and Liverpool looked the better side for much of the game, but Needham came to the rescue in the 70th minute with a fine effort. Another draw, another replay.

Fairly, the venue for the replay, Burnden Park, suited Liverpool fans more as Nottingham had done for United supporters, but Needham and company could take heart from their title win there the previous year.

Due to the referee and linesmen arriving late to the ground, the game kicked off seven minutes late on a hard surface on a sunny day. Liverpool had a 'hurricane-like' wind and the sun behind them for the first half, and took full advantage, calling all of the shots in the opening exchanges, with Morgan going close before Howell forced his former team-mate Foulke to save with a fine dipping shot. United did manage to break away in the 20th minute, and they were convinced that they had scored when Priest's shot was cleared off the line by Dunlop. Following a loud appeal, Liverpool broke to the other end and scored. This, too, was not without controversy, Allan pulling Needham around the neck to prevent him from challenging Walker, who slotted the ball between Foulke's legs; 1-0 to Liverpool.

With the wind at their backs, Liverpool kept attacking, Morgan forcing Foulke to pull off an excellent save, and the offside flag saved United when Walker was through on goal just before half-time.

The Blades started well in the second half, the wind now in their favour, and the first six minutes all took place in the Liverpool half, but then Liverpool advanced towards the United goal and Allan drew a foul out of Boyle just outside of the penalty area. Allan himself scored directly from the kick to put Liverpool two up, despite Foulke getting his fingertips to the ball. United responded to this straight away, Beer turning a Bennett free kick past the Liverpool keeper Storie to make it 2-1 and, after more pressure on the Liverpool defence, Bennett himself scored, his shot going in off the bar; 2-2.

The game was now end to end, and after 73 minutes Liverpool went back ahead, perhaps fortunately, as Robertson looked to be in an offside position. He managed to get a good cross in from the left and Foulke's save from Allan's header rebounded off Boyle, on to the post, and into the net.

Two minutes later, Boyle brought Cox down in the area, Foulke saved Allan's penalty but Cox put the rebound past the unlucky keeper. With 15 minutes to go, Liverpool were 4-2 ahead and looking on course to make it to the final.

Legs were tiring on both sides, but, in the 84th minute, Priest latched on to Thickett's long ball down the left and scored with a long shot that Storie should probably have saved easily. Just a minute later, Priest scored again as he pounced on Storie's parry. Incredibly, the tie was level at 4-4.

A frantic last five minutes saw both keepers making good saves, and Bennett going close, but the referee's whistle took the tie to a second replay. United again had shown great spirit, although were perhaps fortunate in the end and Storie took much of the blame from a Liverpool perspective.

The venue for the second replay was decided to be Fallowfield, Manchester. The capacity of the stadium was 15,000 but over 30,000 turned up and crowd control became impossible. There were so many delays that the game had to be abandoned at half-time, the first half having taken almost two hours to complete due to stoppages. Liverpool had led by an Allan goal at the time. The refix took place at Derby's Baseball Ground. Priest again scored a late goal, this time the only one in a rough game that sent United into the final.

In six and a half games against the Blades this season, Liverpool had scored 11 goals, and Allan had been involved in almost all of them. Sadly, this great opponent was soon after diagnosed with tuberculosis, and died the following October aged just 24.

Liverpool still had the league to concentrate on, and they were level on points at the top going into the last game which, as fate would have it, was an away trip to second-placed Villa. Perhaps the marathon cup battle with United had taken too much out of them, though, as they were on the wrong side of a 5-0 mauling in what was effectively a cup final for the league title. Liverpool would have to wait two more years before their first major trophy. They have won a few more since. United supporters, meanwhile, had a first-ever FA Cup Final to look forward to.

v Derby County 4-1

5

FA Cup Final
15 April 1899
Crystal Palace, London
Attendance: 78,833

SHEFFIELD UNITED	DERBY COUNTY
Foulke	Fryer
Thickett	Methven
Boyle	Staley
Johnson	Cox
Morren	Paterson
Needham	May
Bennett	Arkesden
Beer	Bloomer
Hedley	Bong
Almond	MacDonald
Priest	Allen
Secretary: John Nicholson	Manager: Harry Newbould

United's route to their first cup final was so tough, with the number of replays, and every draw being away to another top-flight team, that there is little surprise that captain Ernest Needham felt this was their year as they travelled to the final. Their opponents, however, had lost the previous year's final to local rivals Forest, 3-1, so were keen to erase the memory. Scoring Derby's only goal in that game was, perhaps, the most famous player of the time, Steve Bloomer.

Bloomer's stats are astounding. In 525 games for Derby, he scored 331 times, and he scored 28 goals in 23 games for England. So legendary in Derby folklore is he, that his name adorns a current Derby fan podcast, *Steve Bloomer's Washing*. He was short in stature and slight in build, good with the ball at his feet, lightning quick and, obviously given his stats, a great finisher.

Games between the Blades and the Rams became a battle of wits between Bloomer and a renowned United defence (with William 'Fatty' Foulke behind them in goal). In their first meetings in 1894/95, Bloomer and Derby came off best, winning both home and away games 4-1, with Bloomer scoring in each, and there was always extra spice to the proceedings when the two teams met.

By the time the first round of the 1899 FA Cup came around, Derby were well out of contention for any league honours but in no relegation danger, so they set out to make amends for the 1898 disappointment and got off to a flying start, beating Second Division Woolwich Arsenal 6-0 away, then disposed of Wolves and Southampton, beating both 2-1.

As United and Liverpool had battled out a semi-final marathon over three (and one abandoned) games, Bloomer helped himself to a hat-trick as Stoke were swept aside and Derby progressed to a second consecutive final. Both teams must have felt their names were on the cup as they made their way to the Crystal Palace stadium in south London.

The United trainers took the team to Skegness ahead of the game. This was the scene of a wager between William Foulke and chairman Tom Bott, who backed trainer Houseley in a 100-yard race against the giant 20st keeper. Foulke won, so Bott had to pay for the whole team to attend a music hall concert.

The final saw, at the time, a record attendance for a football game, with close to 79,000 people cramming into the south London venue, with both cities well represented in the crowd.

United drew some support from Londoners too. This was because in the previous year, as champions, they had played out an entertaining 1-1 draw against amateur team Corinthians in the first 'Charity Shield' game. Their epic run to this final, especially the semi-final marathon against Liverpool, had kept neutrals enthralled. They also had the draw of the great entertainer Foulke between the sticks, and one of the country's greatest players of the era in Needham.

Unitedites were decked out with red-and-white rosettes, or hats in the case of female supporters, and the ground began to fill up from midday onwards. A downpour before kick-off made conditions underfoot difficult for the spectators trying to get a steady foothold on the grassy banks. Hundreds climbed the trees that surrounded the ground, to get a better view of the game. Needham won the toss, and made Derby play against the breeze, with the sun in their eyes and they kicked off as chants of 'play up, t'county' and 'United, United' rang out around the ground.

Despite a lively start by the Blades, in which most of the play took place in the Derby half, the Rams took the lead after 13 minutes. A corner was curled in which resulted in a goalmouth scramble, including an appeal for a foul against a Derby forward, before the ball fell to Bong, who drilled the ball home.

United pressed for an equaliser, Derby keeper Fryer pulling off two good saves in quick succession, although Bong almost scored a second, beating Needham but not Foulke. Needham was orchestrating the match from midfield, and fed Walter Bennett, whose great cross set up Jack Almond with a clear-cut opportunity to score. Almond's header was weak, though, and Fryer was able to save easily.

Both sides were guilty of wasting chances as the half continued. Great play by Bloomer and Arkesden for Derby set up Bong again, but he mishit a shot that would have been a certain goal, and Foulke was able to gather, and at the other end, another lovely cross from Bennett was unrewarded due to poor finishing by Billy Beer.

Just before half-time, Tommy Morren latched upon a Derby clearance and hit a sweet shot that skimmed the crossbar. Despite a great effort by the Sheffield men, Derby went into the interval a goal to the good.

United had a clear plan to contain Bloomer, which was to overwhelm him with numbers whenever he got the ball, and this had restricted his chances in the first half. Early in the second, though, he broke clear of Peter Boyle, the last man, and only had Foulke to beat. Waiting for the huge keeper to come towards him, Bloomer paused, then fired past him, only for his shot to hit the post and go wide.

Soon after, he beat Boyle again, skipping through a tackle to fire from close range. This time, though, there was no beating Foulke, who pulled off a fine save. It was to be Bloomer and Derby's last genuine chance of the game. Soon after, in the 59th minute, Needham crossed, Bennett put his head on the ball ahead of the Derby keeper's fist, and it flew into the net to bring the scores level.

Bennett, who had been top scorer for United in their championship-winning season, was having a superb afternoon on the right. In the 64th minute, he sped down the wing, feeding Beer on the edge side of the area, who blasted a shot which Fryer could only parry. Beer then followed up to knock in the rebound past the flailing Rams keeper to put United ahead. Bennett then set up George Hedley with two good chances. The first, from a cross, was wasted, but, from a 71st minute corner, Hedley forced another parry from Fryer, leaving Almond with a simple touch to make it 3-1.

The game was now pretty much over as a contest, and in the closing minutes it was Priest's turn to score from a Bennett assist for United's fourth, and then the provider almost turned scorer himself with a powerful shot, only for his goal to be overruled for offside. United had won, and spectators burst on to the field of play in order to watch Needham receive the trophy from leader of the Conservative opposition, Arthur Balfour. United had certainly deserved the win, not just on this performance, but also the whole of the cup run, while Derby had been disappointing in the final, and Bloomer had been kept quiet by the Blades' strategy. In the second half the United forwards, Bennett in particular, had been more sharp, more swift, more clever and shown more stamina than their opponents. Back at Bramall Lane, a reserve match was taking place against Attercliffe in the Sheffield Challenge Cup, in front of 2,000 spectators. Great cheers had gone up when telegrams had relayed news of the goals in London to the scoreboard. The cheers could be clearly heard at Wednesday's league game at Olive Grove. The reserves made it a double cup win, winning 5-2.

After a Monday night out at a London music hall, the team brought home the cup by train on the Tuesday, met on Sheaf Street by crowds decked out in red and white as the train arrived in the evening, and a series of horse-drawn carriages led them through the city centre.

After parading up High Street, Fargate, Pinstone Street and the Moor, the parade finally reached Bramall Lane, the famous ground becoming the new temporary home for the famous trophy. This made United only the third team at that point in time, after Preston and Villa, to have won both league and cup trophies.

v The Wednesday 2-0

FA Cup Second Round
19 February 1900
Owlerton
Attendance: 22,000

SHEFFIELD UNITED	THE WEDNESDAY
Foulke	Mallinson
Thickett	Layton
Boyle	Langley
Johnson	Ferrier
Morren	Crawshaw
Needham	Ruddlesdin
Bennett	Brash
Beer	Pryce
Hedley	Lee
Almond	Wright
Priest	Topham
Secretary: John Nicholson	Manager: Arthur Dickinson

The battle for football supremacy in the city of Sheffield is one that has seesawed ever since United were formed. As the 19th century turned into the 20th, the Bramall Lane team held sway. In the previous two seasons, the red-and-white team had won the First Division and FA Cup, while Wednesday had suffered a first-ever relegation.

Over the preceding few years, Wednesday had struggled to keep up with their Sheffield rivals. In 12 league meetings so far, they had won one and lost six. They did become they first Sheffield team to win the FA Cup in 1896, but this was then surpassed by United's league and cup exploits of the following three seasons. Wednesday were also told that they needed to leave their Olive Grove home, as, due to local railway expansion, their lease would not be renewed. There was talk, especially as Wednesday struggled to keep their First Division status, that the club would fold altogether. A share scheme was issued to raise funds for a new ground. There was a plan to buy the Sheaf House ground on Bramall Lane (behind the pub of the same name which still stands to this day), which would have made the two clubs literal neighbours, but eventually a site was secured in Owlerton. This was made ready for the new season, a fresh start for the old club.

The Wednesday 0 Sheffield United 2

On New Year's Day 1900, Wednesday beat Grimsby 2-1 at home, which meant that both teams led their divisions. The only defeat by a Sheffield team so far in the season had come on 30th December as Wednesday lost the local derby at Chesterfield Town. United, buoyed by their cup success in the previous season, had flown out of the traps. They won their first five games, nine of the following 16, and were six points clear of second-placed Aston Villa as January began, matching Preston's record of 22 undefeated games from the beginning of a season.

Focus now turned to the FA Cup, with extra interest at Bramall Lane as United were the current holders. Drawn at home to Second Division Leicester Fosse, who were challenging Wednesday for promotion, United prevailed. Wednesday, too, also beat a fellow promotion challenger, winning 1-0 against Bolton Wanderers.

When the draw for the second round was made in February 1900, there was great excitement in the city when the two Sheffield teams were pitted against each other for the first time in the competition, the tie to be played at Bramall Lane.

So intense and sour were the relations between the two clubs, and sets of supporters, that the *Sheffield Evening Telegraph* wrote, 'There have been many occasions when bigger crowds have been housed on a ground, but none where one has been agitated more violently than will the case tomorrow. One can hope that the excitement will not result any untoward disturbance.' The Saturday of the game had dawned with a light sprinkling of snow, but it came down heavy shortly after kick-off. This had not deterred 32,381 supporters from making their way to the game, but they were eventually disappointed when renowned referee John Lewis was forced to abandon the game after 50 minutes, with no score, and thankfully none of the anticipated trouble either on the pitch or the stands.

The rearranged game was scheduled to take place on the following Thursday, but another snowstorm meant another postponement until the Saturday, and it took a team of volunteers to clear the ground of snow for a third attempt to complete this game.

George Hedley had a goal disallowed for offside before Wednesday's former England forward Fred Spikesley crossed for Brash to score. In the second half, Spikesley was rendered virtually lame after his knee gave way, as United chased an equaliser, which they got through Jack Almond with ten minutes remaining. The game had been a rough one, with 36 free kicks conceded (16 by United, 20 by Wednesday) and still the tie was undecided. The only thing that was certain was that the eventual winners would have a home game against Bury in the third round.

The first Sheffield derby at Owlerton took place two days later, barely time for tempers to cool or wounds to heal. Spikesley along with fellow foward Millar and keeper Massey were all casualties of the first game, and none of them were fit to line up in the replay. United, though, were able to field an unchanged team. Referee Lewis had his hands full again from the start, Wednesday conceding a number of free kicks in the opening ten minutes, and Harry Johnson had to leave the field for a few minutes after a bad foul by Wright. Great chances to score fell to both sides. Hedley looked certain to score before Layton took the ball from him, then William Foulke produced a piece of goalkeeping magic. Wright had shot after a tricky run, but the legendary United keeper had pulled off a one-handed diving save, then somehow managed to block the rebound. Almond missed an open goal as United continued to dominate, but it was during a Wednesday break when George Lee, who had replaced the injured Millar, came together heavily with Harry Thickett and broke his leg. Wednesday, down to ten men, were now forced to play with one back as they finished the first half.

The second half would produce moments that would live long in the Sheffield footballing memory. The half was just two minutes old when the lone defender, Langley, tripped Bennett to concede a penalty. United skipper Needham stepped up and drove a low penalty past Mallinson. Free kick after free kick followed, with both teams to blame for the rough play, resulting in a number of stoppages. Again, Langley fouled Bennett, and then Mallinson and Fred Priest collided, resulting in both of them needing treatment. The football was almost secondary, although Foulke did have to save well from Wright.

Almost immediately following the save, the referee sent off Pryce because of an over-the-top challenge on Hedley. Wednesday were down to nine, although United were unable to take full advantage straight away, as Hedley was off the field recovering from the challenge.

Bennett was still causing Langley problems, and, with five minutes remaining, Langley put in a two-footed challenge against the United forward. The linesman spotted this, and referee Lewis sent him off too to reduce Wednesday to eight. Bennett was unable to continue following the challenge, but this time United were able to capitalise on the extra two men, and Beer scored to put the tie beyond doubt.

There would be many more epic games between United and Wednesday, but perhaps none as nasty, and this was perhaps the lowest point of the relationship between the two clubs. The next round would again take a replay to settle after a 2-2 draw at Bramall Lane, but Bury won at Gigg Lane and would go on to win the cup 4-0 against Southampton in the final.

The league finished in disappointment. As the Sheffield clubs had played out the draw at the Lane, Villa had beaten Notts County 6-2 to take the top spot. Despite United having two games in hand, the Midlands club stayed there for the rest of the season, United finishing two points behind them. Wednesday, meanwhile, would celebrate an immediate return to the top flight by winning the Second Division title.

In the following few years, the Sheffield seesaw would swing in Wednesday's favour for a while, although this could be argued to be the golden period of Sheffield football as whole, with silverware being won by both teams in the first decade of the century. In this epic cup battle though, the Sheffield football rivalry had been at its most bitter, and though United may have been the winner, football was not.

v Southampton 2-1

FA Cup Final Replay
26 April 1902
Crystal Palace, London
Attendance: 34,794

SHEFFIELD UNITED	SOUTHAMPTON
Foulke	Robinson
Thickett	Fry
Boyle	Molyneux
Johnson	Meston
Wilkinson	Bowman
Needham	Lee
Common	Turner, A.
Barnes	Wood
Hedley	Brown
Priest	Chadwick
Lipsham	Turner, J.
Secretary: John Nicholson	Manager: Ernest Arnfield

'Legendary' is an overused word in modern football, but it is certainly one that can be used in connection with the Sheffield United goalkeeper, William 'Fatty' Foulke. He stood 6ft 4in tall, when the average height of a man was almost a foot shorter, and grew in weight from 13 to 24st over his career (at the time of the 1902 cup final, he was 22st 8lb). Foulke was nicknamed the 'Blackwell Giant' after the mining town in Derbyshire from which he hailed. His other, better-known nickname was, of course, 'Fatty'.

United had signed him from his village team in 1894, rescuing him from a life down the coalmine and this had potentially saved him from an early death or maiming, as an explosion in the mine killed seven men and injured many more the following year. He was the first-choice goalkeeper for the club from the day he signed and became a draw for the spectators not only for his excellent goalkeeping, but also for being a great showman and entertainer. Because of his size and strength, knocking him over or, at least, attempting to do so, had almost become a sport in itself for opposition forwards.

In a 4-1 win at Goodison Park, for instance, the Everton forward John Bell seemed to have only this on his mind, but Foulke landed on top of him in the attempt, and the squashed Toffee had to be carried off. The Everton supporters spent much of the rest of the game trying to hit Foulke with stones.

Foulke was never shy of expressing an opinion, either. After the 1899 FA Cup Final, the former miner would tell the *Sheffield Independent* that he 'didn't think much of Mr. Balfour,' the Conservative party leader who had presented the trophy to winning captain Ernest Needham.

It is, perhaps, a travesty that Foulke won just one England cap, and that one was at Bramall Lane (at the time, the home ground committee picked the team). Perhaps his comments and antics had something to do with this. Brian Clough, for example, proved years later that ability matters less than compliance when it comes to the FA.

Some stories, like Foulke himself, grew with the telling. There are tales of him pulling down the crossbar when bored, and it is even claimed that the song 'Who Ate All the Pies' was created about him!

United had reached their second cup final in 1901, only to lose in a replay at Burnden Park against Southern League team Tottenham Hotspur. Renewing their cup exploits in 1902, the club reached its third final in four seasons. After disposing of fledgling Southern League club Northampton Town 2-0 at the County Ground, and then beating Bolton 2-1 at Bramall Lane, the quarter-finals saw them drawn against the 'other' United, of Newcastle, at the time the only other team in the league to share the name. After a drawn game at St. James' Park, an excellent replay resulted in a 2-1 win, and set up yet another encounter with Derby and their talismanic striker, Steve Bloomer. It took two replays for United to again prove to be the Rams' cup nemesis. Despite missing Needham through injury in the second replay, a Fred Priest goal proved to be enough to take United to the final.

Their opponents would be Southern League club Southampton, who had been runners-up in 1900. The final took place on 19 April, under hot sun, and was, by all accounts, a dull game. Alf Common, a forward signed from Sunderland the previous season and who had scored the winner against Newcastle, gave United the lead in the 55th minute. He, and Walter Bennett, were reduced by injury to passenger status, and the game was petering to a close when controversy struck in the 88th minute.

Turner had played a ball in from the wing to Wood, standing in a clearly offside position in front of Foulke. Wood (who would later admit his offside position) instinctively put the ball in the net, and Foulke made no attempt to save it knowing it was offside, and proving the maxim 'play to the whistle'. The team, and the crowd, were stunned when referee Kirkham awarded the goal after discussion with the linesman. They claimed that the ball had touched Peter Boyle, the United defender, on the way to Wood, which Boyle strongly denied. Regardless, the goal stood, and the game was drawn.

Tempers flared, resulting in an altercation between a Southampton supporter and Needham as the teams left the field, but a more legendary tale is that of Foulke, still angered at the decision, and determined to confront the referee. On the advice of his linesman, Mr Kirkham wisely locked his door as a stark-naked Foulke approached, and waited for him to leave before making an escape.

The replay took place the following Saturday, again at the Crystal Palace. The crowds for replays had always been smaller than the original match, and this was no exception. A second London trip in a week was too much for many Unitedites, but they were 'well represented' in a crowd of 34,794. Also represented were the recently arrived Australian cricket team, ahead of an Ashes summer, accompanied to the game by a certain W. G. Grace.

As both teams' usual colours were identical (even down to the blue(!) shorts and socks), and Southampton had worn the red and white in the first game, United now took to the field in the stripes.

Bennett, the hero of the 1899 final, was still injured, so Common was moved to the right wing with Billy Barnes taking his place as inside-right. As the game began, Barnes tested the Southampton keeper early, then Southampton broke and Lee shot wide.

From a huge goal kick from Foulke, assisted by the wind, the ball was crossed into the Southampton danger area. Robinson, the Southampton keeper misjudged the flight, came for the cross, slipped, and George Hedley put the ball into the open goal. Only two minutes of the game had passed.

An incident in the first half caused Common to receive some poor treatment from the crowd for the remainder of the game.

Retrieving a ball that had gone out of play, a spectator, probably accidentally, kicked Common's foot, who proceeded to give the youth a slap across the face.

Despite having the wind at their backs, United's advantage was countered with the sun in their eyes, and the game became scrappy. A few half chances fell to both sides, but United held their one-goal advantage until half-time.

The second half began with the ball moving from end to end, Wood forcing a good save from Foulke then Common doing the same to Robinson. After 70 minutes, Southampton were level. An excellent cross from Turner on the left caused real problems for United. In the scramble, Brown slashed at the ball, which went into the top corner, Foulke having no chance of stopping the ball.

This gave Southampton renewed vigour. C. B. Fry (who also played cricket for England, and had once held a British long-jump record) and Turner in particular caused problems, but Foulke was equal to anything thrown at him. In one attempt, Wood was adjudged to have handled the ball. From the free kick, United worked the ball to Needham on the edge of the area on the left. Needham's dropping shot caused Robinson to fumble the ball into the path of Barnes, who chested it into the net; 79 minutes gone, and United led.

They would not throw away the lead a second time. The backs remained solid, and Southampton's response was limited to a speculative long-range effort by Fry. For the second time in four years, United had won the FA Cup.

After a night in a St Pancras hotel with a victory meal, the United party would take the train to Derby for a league match on the Monday. With little at stake for either team, and thoughts perhaps of the victory parade later that evening, United lost 3-1 in front of just 5,000 spectators. They then caught the train to Sheffield, to be hailed by a crowd of between 20,000 and 30,000 outside of the Town Hall.

One of the last acts of United's season, in the Derby game, had been Foulke pulling off a 'supreme save' from Steve Bloomer, two genuine footballing legends of the Victorian game facing one another yet again.

v Bradford City 7-3

Football League First Division
4 March 1912
Bramall Lane
Attendance: 5,500

SHEFFIELD UNITED	BRADFORD CITY
Mitchell	Spendiff
Sturgess	Campbell
Benson	Boocock
Brelsford	Hampton
Wilkinson	Hargreaves
Trueman	McDonald
Kitchen	Bond
Simmons	Spiers
Gillespie	Walden
Hardinge	McIlvenny
Revill	Logan
Secretary: John Nicholson	Manager: Peter O'Rourke

While United had gone out of the 1911 FA Cup to Second Division Chelsea, Bradford City set out to defend the trophy they had won the previous season. After progressing to the third round, their reward was an away derby match at neighbours Bradford Park Avenue, which necessitated the moving of their league visit to Bramall Lane to a Monday afternoon. With both United and Bradford safely ensconced in mid-table, City's attention still on the cup, a Monday afternoon kick-off, and torrential rain, just 5,500 turned out to watch the match.

It would turn out to be one of those 'I was there' games, memorable games played out before low crowds (see the Chester and Brighton games elsewhere in this book). Perhaps the United team of 1912 preferred the quieter crowds, as the previous Monday's game against Manchester City had attracted an even lower attendance, 5,000, and had finished 6-2.

Scoring a hat-trick in that game had been Billy Gillespie. The Ulster-born forward had recently signed from Second Division Leeds City for £500, scoring on his debut at Newcastle on Boxing Day, and had scored six goals in 12 games by the time of the Bradford City refix in March. Bradford came into the game after a 1-0 win over championship-challengers Everton two days earlier, and had the best defensive record in the league, having conceded just 28 goals in 27 games. Few expected the Blades to score many against them then, especially as they may have had one eye on the next match, the Sheffield derby at Owlerton.

United had been inconsistent throughout the season, though, so nobody really knew what to expect when they watched them play. The league campaign had started well, a 3-2 win at Oldham, but then Bolton delivered a 5-0 hammering in the first home game. Much chopping and changing of the team followed, resulting in just nine goals being scored in the next 13 games. A first-ever relegation looked a strong possibility, but then came a remarkable run of form, helped in part by the signing of Gillespie. From seven games, five were won, 18 goals scored and United lifted themselves clear of danger. On the morning of the Bradford game, heavy rain fell on Sheffield, resulting in a quagmire of a pitch. Bradford had rested six of their key players ahead of their quarter-final against Barnsley. United were virtually full-strength apart from an injury to their first-choice keeper Joe Lievesley, with reserve keeper Joe Mitchell making just his eighth appearance in three seasons for the club.

United kicked the game off, and within seconds had a penalty, after Campbell was adjudged to have handled the ball. Bob Benson, with a 30-yard run-up, smashed the ball past Spendiff in the Bradford goal.

Seven minutes later, the Blades were two ahead. Wally Hardinge playing a ball behind the Bradford backs for Gillespie to run on to. He took the ball past half-back Hargreaves, who slipped in the mud, and ran through the gap between the last two defenders before firing into the top corner from ten yards.

Bradford then had a good chance, Bob Benson charging down a hard shot from Bond, while Hardinge and Kitchen both went close for the Blades. Shortly before half-time, United had another penalty, after Hargreaves pushed Gillespie. Benson took the responsibility again and, although his run-up was less pronounced, put it away.

The second half began and was only four minutes old when Hardinge flicked a ball on from a corner, for Gillespie to head home to put United 4-0 up.

Bradford had their best effort then. Spiers fed Walden, who ran between Benson and Albert Sturgess. Walden's shot from the edge of the area beat Mitchell, only to go a foot outside of the post.

The Blades' defence was finally breached in the 56th minute, with what was probably the goal of the game, scored by Spiers (who had scored Bradford's winning goal in the previous year's FA Cup Final). Spiers latched on to a pass from Hampton and fired the ball into the top corner of Mitchell's net.

In the 63rd minute, Hardinge again fed Gillespie, who, just as he had done a week earlier, completed a hat-trick. There was little time to celebrate, though, as Bradford scored straight from the restart, this time through Walden, an amateur who had represented Britain in that summer's Olympic games. The small crowd must have been thankful of the scoreboard to remind them of the score at this point (it was 5-2 if you're also struggling to keep total), and it wasn't long before the operator was having to change it again. On 68 minutes, Hardinge dribbled the ball through the Bradford defence and unleashed a shot which rebounded from the crossbar and landed at the feet of Joe Kitchen for a simple tap-in. Hardinge had provided four assists, not bad for a player who was considered surplus to requirements and transfer-listed a few weeks earlier. (Kitchen was better known nationally as a cricketer, playing 623 first-class games for Kent as an all-rounder and appearing in an Ashes test in 1921). After Kitchen had put away Hardinge's rebound, Walden again scored straight from the restart (6-3) and, with 15 minutes to go, Jimmy Simmons's mazy dribble allowed him to set up Gillespie, who scored his fourth and his team's seventh from long range.

Though the second half had averaged a goal every four minutes to this point, this turned out to be the last one of this incredible game. The final score, United 7 Bradford City 3.

Bradford's ploy of fielding a weakened side failed not only in the context of this game but also in terms of their quarter-final. After playing out three 0-0 draws with Barnsley, a third replay at Bramall Lane went to extra time before City lost 3-2. The final would also go to a replay, which would be played at Bramall Lane, Barnsley winning for it the only time in their history.

After a 1-1 draw against The Wednesday the Saturday after the Bradford game, United continued their high-scoring streak at Bramall Lane, including a 6-1 win over Manchester United, which meant that their final six home games saw a total of 25 goals scored. The following season, though, poor away form and a porous defence would lead to another mid-table finish, which was typical of this period of United's history. The golden years of the Ernest Needham era may have passed, but the Blades were still capable of providing some memorable moments, and this game against Bradford would be long remembered.

v Chelsea 3-0

FA Cup Final
24 April 1915
Old Trafford, Manchester
Attendance: 49,557

SHEFFIELD UNITED	CHELSEA
Gough	Molyneux
Cook	Bettridge
English	Harrow
Sturgess	Taylor
Brelsford	Logan
Utley	Walker
Simmons	Ford
Fazackerley	Halse
Kitchen	Thomson
Masterman	Croal
Evans	McNeil
Secretary: John Nicholson	Manager: David Calderhead

The Blades had been unlucky in the 1913/14 season not to reach the FA Cup Final, a disputed Burnley goal ending their challenge in the semi-final, the Blades' first-ever defeat at that stage in the cup. After that defeat, United won five league games in a row as the season drew to a close, so there was genuine optimism going into the new season. Everything, though, was soon overshadowed by the declaration of war against Germany three weeks before the season kicked off.

There was a general feeling in the country that the war would be over by Christmas, so the footballing authorities, encouraged by the Government for morale purposes, pressed on with the original fixture lists. By the spring, though, no end to war was in sight. The FA Cup Final was played two days after the first use of poison gas in a war, by the German army at Ypres. Little surprise, then, that league and cup seasons were postponed after the season had wrapped up.

While the war provided ample enough grounds for pessimism and despair, United had done little to lift their supporters' spirits in the first two months of the season. They won just two of their first 12 games, and they were two points from the relegation places. To make matters worse, star player Billy Gillespie's leg was broken in the opening game against Sunderland, and he would play no further part in the season. A home win against Liverpool in November, however, sparked a great run of form that, by March, saw them just four points off top team Manchester City with two games in hand. The form also carried into the cup, and there was now genuine talk of being just the third club, after Preston and Villa, to achieve a league and cup double. In the cup, after a win at Blackpool, there followed four ties against top-flight teams. Liverpool and Bradford Park Avenue were both beaten 1-0 at Bramall Lane, but the quarter-final draw was a tough one, away at Oldham, who were, at that point, second in the league. The Blades were fortunate to earn a draw, Oldham hitting the bar, but made no mistake in the replay, being two up at half-time and winning 3-0, before disposing of Bolton 2-1 in the semi-final at Ewood Park to reach their fourth FA Cup Final.

Their opponents would be Chelsea, a fledgling club formed as a pet project for a London businessman, Gus Mears, just ten years earlier. Mears had bankrolled Chelsea (sound familiar?) to the top flight within two years, although it would be another four decades before they would be genuine title challengers. Chelsea seemed to relish their underdog status in the cup, having beaten league-chasing Manchester City, then Newcastle and Everton en route, and this underdog status had not prevented Barnsley, Bradford City or Wolves from lifting the trophy in recent finals. With two games remaining in the league, though, they had more than the cup on their minds, being in a relegation dogfight, while United's title challenge had been ended by a defeat at Liverpool. As usual cup final venue Crystal Palace had been taken over by the Royal Navy for war work, the final was held at Old Trafford, only the second time that a (non-replay) final had been held outside of the capital. Nobody knew it at the time, but Crystal Palace had held its last final.

On the morning, Old Trafford was, eerily fitting considering the events taking place a few hundred miles away at Ypres, shrouded in a thick yellow smog, and there was genuine concern that the game would not be able to take place. The fog was accompanied by rain, and, fittingly, the atmosphere was gloomy and oppressive. As the *Sunday Mirror* reported, 'There was little of the enthusiasm usually associated with the final,' although close to 50,000 had still turned up to watch the game. Many of the spectators were already enlisted, and in uniform, so much so that the game would become dubbed the 'Khaki Final'.

United's success had been built on a sound defence, with both teams having similar scoring records, so it was felt that the pressure was on Chelsea's back line to perform if they were to get anything out of the cup final.

The opening exchanges saw attacks by both teams. The Blades' Joe Kitchen put two early efforts wide, but then Chelsea got some momentum, Jack English having to clear after a scramble from a corner kick. United attacked, Kitchen's 20-yard drive saved by Molyneux in the Chelsea goal. Croal then played a lovely cross into the United box but no forward could get on to the end of it and, at the opposite end, Kitchen tested Molyneux again, this time from a tight angle which was tipped wide.

Bob Evans got away on the left and put in a glorious cross to Stanley Fazackerley, who missed the ball. This distracted the Chelsea keeper, and fortunately for the Blades, it fell to Jimmy Simmons who hit it first time into the goal; 35 minutes gone, United led, and they took the lead to the interval after a fairly even first half.

The mist started to thicken over half-time, as the band played 'It's a Long Way to Tipperary', and it worsened as the second half got underway. From each end of the ground, the only thing that could be seen from the crowd behind the opposite goal was the occasional flicker of matches lighting cigarettes.

Chelsea never looked like levelling the game in the second half. The Blades had Wally Masterman's goal disallowed for offside, while captain George Utley commanded the middle of the park, breaking up most Chelsea moves then distributing the ball well to the forwards. Many had attributed the general improvement in United's play in this season to the signing of Utley from Barnsley for £2,000, not least his wonderful solo goal that had won the semi-final. Modern Unitedites used to seeing the club scrimping and saving will be astounded to discover that his signing was a world-record transfer fee at the time!

Chelsea had their keeper, Molyneux, to thank for keeping the score down to 1-0 for so long, pulling off some great saves, one in particular from a goalbound Masterman header but, with seven minutes to go, he was finally beaten again, Masterman smashing the ball into Chelsea's crossbar and the ball landing at the feet of Stanley Fazackerley, who slotted home.

Just four minutes later, Kitchen dribbled through the Chelsea defence to score United's third, causing a pitch invasion from delighted Unitedites. Shortly after the field was cleared of the interlopers, the referee blew his whistle. Sheffield United had won the FA Cup for a third time.

Presenting the trophy, Lord Derby finished with a reminder that 'we have got our duty in front of us' to 'play with one another for England now.'

As the cup final was being played out, so was a full programme of Football League games. Chelsea now had to play two league games in three days, the last of which was a winner-takes-all relegation game against Notts County. Chelsea lost 2-0, and so had lost the cup final and were relegated in the space of five days. The game would be the last First Division action anywhere for nearly five years.

Of the 22 players who took to the field for the final, 11 would see active service during the war. Miraculously, given the massive loss of life in the war, none of them perished, although United's reserve left-winger Jimmy Revill was killed in France in 1917.

The day after the cup final, Allied troops landed at Gallipoli.

v The Wednesday 3-2

FA Cup Second Round
31 January 1925
Bramall Lane
Attendance: 40,256

SHEFFIELD UNITED	THE WEDNESDAY
Sutcliffe	Brown
Cook	Inglis
Birks	Felton
Pantling	Toone
King	Wilson
Green	Powell
Mercer	Lowdell
Sampy, T.	Hill
Johnson	Trotter
Gillespie	Taylor
Tunstall	Richardson
Secretary: John Nicholson	Manager: Robert Brown

Having spent just two seasons of their league history in different divisions, the two Sheffield clubs were separated again by Wednesday's second relegation in 1920. Unlike the previous relegation, where Wednesday had bounced straight back, this was to be a longer time apart.

Wednesday for a period became a mid-table team in the second tier, just as United were in the first, so there was great anticipation when the two teams were drawn together in the FA Cup in 1925 for their first meeting in a major competition in five years.

The game was to be one of the most memorable for a generation of Sheffield football supporters. In the previous season United had, for the first time since the First World War, been in with an outside chance of the league title for a good proportion of the season. Only Sunderland had outscored them, but at the end of the season, it was former United player Herbert Chapman's Huddersfield who would take the championship trophy home, a 1-0 win at Bramall Lane effectively ending the Blades' challenge.

At the beginning of the 1924/25 season, United went through a goalkeeping crisis. Having terminated the contract of goalkeeper Harold Gough for breach of FA regulations (by owning a pub) after 11 years with the club, they were forced to try three different keepers, the last being Charlie Sutcliffe, signed out of sheer desperation for an over-the-odds fee from Rotherham County. By the end of November, United had conceded 30 goals in 17 games and were only clear of the relegation positions on goal average, but a mini-revival over the Christmas period meant that thoughts of relegation had all but vanished by the time the cup meeting against Wednesday came around at the end of January. In the ten preceding league games, only one was lost, 2-0 at Notts County, and even then, only because Fred Tunstall had missed two penalties. Wednesday, meanwhile, were well out of the promotion race by January, so the cup had become even more important to keeping the season alive for both clubs.

Expecting a huge crowd, United had moved the pitch eight yards closer to the cricket pavilion to allow spectators to use that side of the ground. United were hoping for a record attendance, but the weather was atrocious. Still, over 40,000 spectators came out to watch the game (for context, the Boxing Day fixture against Sunderland had brought out four thousand more).

The weather not only had an impact on the attendance, but also on conditions. The pitch was a quagmire, although the rain had eased off by the time that the game began.

Any fears that the mud and water would result in the teams taking it easy were soon quashed. Wednesday, kicking towards the Shoreham Street end with the wind behind them, attacked. Hill played a ball through to Trotter who, as he was challenged by Len Birks, stroked the ball into the net, just inside the right post. Only five minutes had passed, and it took just four more for Trotter to get a second. Lowdell crossed from the right, George Green misread the flight of the ball, which left Trotter with a free header which he snapped up. Nine minutes gone, and Wednesday were two up.

Despite the good start, Wednesday manager Brown changed the tactics which had served them well in the opening exchanges, and they now became guilty of hanging on to the ball for too long. This gave United the chance to win the ball in the muddy conditions, and they began to exploit this, pulling a goal back in the 13th minute. Fred Tunstall played a ball through to Tommy Sampy, which a Wednesday defender failed to clear, and Sampy knocked in the ball from close range. For Sampy, whose younger brother Bill also played for United, this was his first goal of the season. Soon after, a shot from Billy Gillespie hit the post. In the next attack, Harold Pantling sent the ball into the box. Gillespie cleverly dummied, allowing the ball to go between his legs and into the path of George Green who, stronger on his left foot, twisted this leg behind his right and back-heeled it into the net. It was a wonderful goal and, amazingly, after just 15 minutes, the game was level at 2-2.

It was all United now, their superiority in technique and stamina clearly showing. The rain had started to come down heavily again. Brown, in the Wednesday goal, was making save after excellent save to keep the scores level. The post, too, came to Wednesday's rescue, the mud playing a part as it caused Harry Johnson's ground shot to swerve into the upright.

Sampy, in the right inside-forward role, was linking up well with David Mercer on the right wing. Both of them had been regular fixtures in the team until a year earlier, and were back in the team today due to injuries, an old partnership reinstated.

As the light was fading fast, the referee ordered that there would be no half-time interval, merely an immediate change of end. United now had the wind behind them, and it took just 90 seconds for them to take advantage of this and establish a lead for the first time in the match. Johnson, son of the United trainer and former player (also Harry), and on his way to becoming the club record-goalscorer, found he was running into a dead-end of defenders. He fed the ball to Sampy. Running wide to the right, Sampy suddenly cut inside and shot from an angle, the ball going high and wide of the keeper and into the Wednesday goal.

The game was still being played at a fast pace, despite the conditions, and United launched attack after attack, Brown coming to Wednesday's rescue again saving a close-range effort from Mercer, and Gillespie put a shot just wide of the post. Wednesday's post was then rattled again, this time by Gillespie, although it would not have counted as Johnson was in an offside position.

For a moment, it looked like United's pressure was going to go unrewarded, as Hill made a superb dribble past three Blades defenders before shooting. Sutcliffe, to United's relief, was able to tip the ball over the bar. This was to be Wednesday's last effort. Both teams were tiring in the conditions, and United wound the clock down to emerge as winners, to book a home tie against Everton in the following Monday's draw.

Wednesday, meanwhile, went on a slump which saw them win just four more games in the season, and at one point looking like they might get sucked into a relegation scrap to the third tier. In the end, they survived by four points.

The *Star Green 'Un* described the game as one that 'will go down in history as one of the best, if not the best, game which has ever taken place between United and The Wednesday.'

Every Blade has their favourite derby game, hopefully all captured in this book. For supporters between the world wars, this was theirs.

v Cardiff City 1-0

FA Cup Final
25 April 1925
Empire Stadium, Wembley, London
Attendance: 91,763

SHEFFIELD UNITED	CARDIFF CITY
Sutcliffe	Farquharson
Cook	Nelson
Milton	Blair
Pantling	Wake
King	Keenor
Green	Hardy
Mercer	Davies
Boyle	Gill
Johnson	Nicholson
Gillespie	Beadles
Tunstall	Evans
Secretary: John Nicholson	Manager: Fred Stewart

The 'Empire Stadium' at Wembley, built to form part of the 1924/25 British Empire Exhibition, was completed on 24 April 1923, four days before the FA Cup Final of that year. This final would go down in history as the 'White Horse Final', as an estimated 300,000 supporters attempted to see the game, the crowd somehow being kept off the pitch by police on horses, one of which became the defining image of the game.

The game was played between Bolton and West Ham, but it could have just as easily been the Blades and the Hammers. In the semi-final against Bolton, United had gone down to ten men early in the game through injury, and lost by a single, mishit fluke of a goal.

They only had to wait two more years, though, to get their first Wembley trip. Tommy Sampy had come into the side to replace the injured Tommy Boyle and had scored two in the second-round game against Wednesday. He had appeared in every round after this, but he lost his place again to Boyle by the time the final came around. (Boyle's father, Peter, had been an FA Cup winner twice with United).

It was Fred Tunstall who was the real star of the route to Wembley, scoring in every round after the Wednesday game. Signed from non-league Scunthorpe in 1920, he was an inside-left who could whip in great crosses while sprinting at great speed. Capped for the first time against Scotland at Hampden Park in 1923, he provided the crosses for both England goals on debut, and he won seven caps in total. He would make 437 appearances for United.

Tunstall had scored the only goal, a blistering shot, at home to Everton in the third round and the first goal in a 2-0 win over West Brom in the quarter-final. The goal, scored at the Bramall Lane end of the ground, was captured on film by *Pathe News* and can today be found on the internet. It is worth seeking out.

The semi-final pitted United against Second Division Southampton at Stamford Bridge. United had Southampton right-back Tom Parker to thank as he sliced the ball into his own goal shortly before half-time, then hit a penalty straight at Sutcliffe shortly after the interval. Southampton were then punished further as Tunstall pounced on hesitation by the backs and drove the ball home to book United's first Wembley trip.

Their opponents would be Cardiff, who were the first Welsh club to reach an FA Cup Final. After the events of the 1923 final, the cup final had become an all-ticket match, and the debacle that is cup final ticket allocation had begun. There was unhappiness in the build-up to the final that Cardiff were able to acquire a larger proportion of tickets, particularly in the General Admission areas (costing two pence per ticket), than their Sheffield rivals despite the Blades commanding a much larger support across the season. As Cardiff were the first Welsh club to reach the final, much press talk was about this game being an England v Wales tie, taking on even more significance than ever, despite the Cardiff team containing only four Welshmen and being managed by an Englishman. The railway companies reported that 140,000 people used the special excursion trains, with 91,763 taking their places in the stadium, the rest participating in the festivities and wearing rosettes and badges (and leeks in the case of Cardiff fans) in the streets of the capital.

Writing after the game, the *Sheffield Daily Telegraph* 'London Correspondent' bemoaned the all-ticket policy and increased percentage of seating areas, missing the 'old traditions' and atmosphere, in much the same way that many today complain about modern all-seater stadia. 'Men who are so methodical as to book their seats well in advance,' he wrote, 'are not usually of the kind which abandons itself to the emotions. They seemed ... less ferocious in their feelings towards the other side's players than they should have been.'

Ten years after the Blades had last won the cup, the team were greeted on the Wembley turf by the Duke of York, later King George VI, accompanied by Charles Clegg, a man who had been instrumental in the formation of both Sheffield clubs and was now President of the FA.

The game began, and United showed very early what their gameplan was, to play lightning-quick football, and, to use modern terms, a pressing game. When Cardiff had the ball, the Blades gave them no time to settle, their backs swooping as if from nowhere, and then releasing their forwards. The ball was never allowed to stop when United were in possession, moving from wing to wing to centre and back again.

It was this kind of play that led to United taking the lead. Tommy Boyle and David Mercer passed the ball swiftly back and forth between them on the right, drawing the Cardiff backs out of position, before a high, swinging cross was put into the box. The cross caught the Cardiff defender Wake in two minds, either to move towards the ball or wait for it to come to him. He chose the latter, but the moment's indecision was enough for Tunstall, flying in from the left, to get the slightest of touches, taking it out of the defender's path and leaving himself with a simple finish. The roar from the crowd was deafening as Tunstall wheeled away in celebration.

United continued to attack, although the early pace was so quick as to be unsustainable. Billy Gillespie struck a beauty, only to see it glance off a team-mate's leg, Tunstall shot just over and both Boyle and Harry Johnson went close.

In the second half, Johnson again had a good chance and was pushed off the ball with what seemed to be a Cardiff arm, but no penalty was forthcoming. Another penalty shout, this time against Blair, also went unrewarded.

In the dying minutes, United supporters had cause to fear that all of their team's good work would be in vain, as an almighty goalmouth scramble took place in the Blades' area. Ernest Milton half-cleared, former Wednesday striker Gill picked up on the loose ball, took a few touches, wheeled, and was tackled by Milton. The ball found its way to Nicholson, who was able to get the shot away. Wide.

Again, the Welsh side attacked, and again a scramble ensued, United struggling desperately to clear, until Tunstall appeared on the scene and booted it upfield. The Cardiff threat was repelled, United had won their fourth FA Cup and the famous trophy was staying in England, at least for a few more years.

After receiving the cup from the Duke of York, there was little time for the United team to celebrate. On the Monday, the team played Everton in a dead rubber at Goodison Park, drawing 1-1. The only one of the cup-winning team not to play in this game was Milton.

After staying overnight in Liverpool, they caught a train, decked out in red and white, to Victoria Station (opposite where the Victoria Holiday Inn hotel now stands) where they were met by an open-top bus to take them to the Town Hall, through crowds of thousands. All other traffic and trams were forced to a halt. As the procession went up High Street, fireworks were set off from the roof of the *Sheffield Telegraph* offices on the corner of York Street.

After a Town Hall stop, the procession then continued to Bramall Lane, via the Moor, where a local butcher stopped the bus to give each member of the team a leg of mutton!

Matchwinner Tunstall got the most adulation, being showered in confetti by female supporters. His goal had won the cup for United. Surely nobody could have predicted that only one other player would ever score for United at the old Wembley Stadium again, Alan Cork in 1993, or that this would be the last major trophy the club would win?

v Cardiff City 11-2

Football League First Division
1 January 1926
Bramall Lane
Attendance: 21,943

SHEFFIELD UNITED	CARDIFF CITY
Alderson	Farquharson
Sampy, W.	Nelson
Birks	Blair
Sampy, T.	Hardy
Waugh	Sloan
Green	Nicholson
Mercer	Davies, W.
Boyle	Davies, L.
Johnson	Ferguson
Gillespie	Cassidy
Tunstall	McLachlan
Secretary: John Nicholson	Manager: Fred Stewart

As FA Cup holders United closed out a successful 1925, they were the top scorers in the First Division, scoring 56 goals in 23 games, which was already one more than they had scored in the entirety of the previous season.

There had been a change in the summer to the offside law, reducing the number of defenders required for an attacker to be played onside, from three to the current-day two, and United's pacy forwards were able to exploit this. By the end of December, three players had already achieved double-figure goal tallies – Harry Johnson, Fred Tunstall and Bert Menlove. As other defences struggled to get to grips with the new law, though, so too did the Blades. Just two teams conceded more than them in the season and so, not surprisingly, there were many high-scoring games. United lost 7-4 at Bury in September, and the following month beat Manchester City 8-3 at Bramall Lane, with Johnson scoring four goals.

A huge defensive reorganisation took place. Goalkeeper Jack Alderson was bought from Crystal Palace, Bill Sampy promoted from the reserves, while his brother Tommy was moved back to right-half, although these measures never really fixed the problem.

Cardiff travelled to Bramall Lane on New Year's Day hoping to avenge their April FA Cup Final defeat. The Welshmen had made an indifferent start to the season, hovering above the relegation places but picking up enough wins to remain outside of any real danger. The weather was miserable, cold and wet, and the pitch was incredibly muddy, but United had earned a reputation as 'mudlarks', so would have gone into the game with a huge amount of confidence, and nearly 22,000 braved the weather expecting to see a good game. They would not be disappointed.

The scoring began after 14 minutes. The ball was played into the Cardiff area, where a defender appeared to handle the ball. The referee ignored the protest for a penalty, but Billy Gillespie was able to get on to the ball anyway and fired it into the net. After 22 minutes it was 2-0, Johnson setting up Tommy Boyle, who unleashed a powerful shot past Cardiff keeper Farquharson.

Cardiff's forwards had done very little by this point, but now chased a way back into the game. In the 30th minute, McLachlan's effort hit the post, but Willie Davies was able to score from the rebound.

The Blades' two-goal advantage was restored just four minutes later, David Mercer breaking down the right touchline and putting in a wonderful cross for Harry Johnson to head home. Mercer himself got in the scoring act in the 40th minute, cutting inside from the right with the ball before shooting with his left. The Cardiff keeper got his hands to it, but the slippery conditions saw it slip through his hands and over the line. The unfortunate custodian let the same thing happen again in the 43rd minute, again from Mercer, who drilled the ball towards goal from the right edge of the area. At half-time, United led 5-1. If Cardiff looked like they were already beaten, another nail in their coffin followed early in the second half, as Blair injured his foot which reduced them to ten men. United continued to press, and made it 6-1 after 53 minutes, Gillespie heading in Tunstall's cross from the left. United's seventh came from Johnson two minutes later.

After 71 minutes, Mercer completed his hat-trick. A technically gifted player with accurate crossing ability, United had paid a British record transfer fee of £4,500 for him from Hull in 1920, and he had won two England caps in 1922/23, scoring in a 6-1 win over Belgium at Highbury. His brother, Arthur, would make his United debut in the 1926/27 season.

Mercer's third goal against Cardiff was the first of three goals scored in under five minutes for United. Boyle got his second, and United's ninth, then Tunstall's powerful angled drive took United into double figures in the 76th minute.

United's final goal came with ten minutes remaining. Farquharson rushed out to tackle the oncoming Johnson but missed, and Johnson was able to slot the ball into an empty net to complete his hat-trick. This completed United's scoring, but Cardiff did manage to score in the 87th minute through Len Davies. They could, though, have had more in the game, with at least three good chances wasted.

United had very little chance to celebrate the huge victory, as they had to travel to Goodison Park for a meeting with Everton the next day, which ended 1-1. They finished the season in fifth place, that leaky defence preventing any real challenge for the title. The goals in the Cardiff game contributed to United breaking a league scoring record of 102 goals for a 42-game season, which stood until 1930 when Wednesday scored 105. This only lasted for a season, though, as Villa romped to 128 goals in the next campaign.

The 11-2 win is a record for a league match in Sheffield. Incidentally, in the Cardiff travelling party, but not selected to play, was a player called Alf Hagan, who had a young son by the name of Jimmy.

v Burnley 10-0
Football League First Division
19 January 1929
Bramall Lane
Attendance: 23,280

SHEFFIELD UNITED	BURNLEY
Wharton	Somerville
Partridge	McCluggage
Birks	Waterfield
Sampy, T.	Steel
Matthews	Hunt
Green	Parkin
Gibson	Bruton
Phillipson	Stage
Johnson	Beel
Gillespie	Devine
Tunstall	Freeman
Secretary: John Nicholson	Manager: Albert Pickles

United's seasons in the 1920s were, by and large, a story of mid-table finishes with the occasional cup run (including the FA Cup win in 1925). The team never really challenged for the title, but were never really in any danger of being relegated. Consistent for the team in the decade was 'Young' Harry Johnson. He was the son of the United trainer, 'Old' Harry, who had won a league championship and two FA Cup winners' medals with United two decades earlier, as well as six England caps.

'Young' Harry had got his opportunity with United at 16, as the Blades were putting out makeshift teams during the First World War, and he impressed from the beginning. By the time the war had ended and football resumed, he had cemented a place in the first team. He was top league and cup scorer for nine consecutive seasons in the 1920s, including a tally of 43 goals in 44 games in 1927/28. Surprisingly, Johnson was never selected to play for England, while at the same time, his team-mate Tunstall won seven caps. The reason for this was probably timing, in that he would have to displace two genuine legends of the game to win a cap, Villa's Billy Walker, and later, Everton's William 'Dixie' Dean. Johnson's 150th league goal had come as the first of a hat-trick against Newcastle in the first home game of the 1928/29 season. He scored another hat-trick against Manchester United on the Boxing Day to bring his total number of league and cup hat-tricks to 19.

Just over two weeks later, the Blades travelled to Turf Moor to take on fellow mid-table team Burnley in the third round of the cup. They were keen to have a cup run similar to the previous season, when a narrow semi-final second replay defeat to Huddersfield had shattered dreams of a second Wembley trip in three years. Burnley had their own ideas, and United were missing Johnson, laid up sick in bed with a heavy cold. While perhaps a draw may have been a better reflection of the performance, Burnley, as they had done in the league meeting at Turf Moor in the September, won 2-1.

In one of those coincidences that the fixture list often throws up, United had a chance for revenge just a week after the cup defeat, and the Clarets made the return journey to Bramall Lane for the league meeting. Johnson was fit again, and Burnley would have not forgotten the last time that they faced him at Bramall Lane, when he scored a hat-trick in a 5-2 win. Burnley were without Page, their match-winner from the cup game, who had picked up a leg injury. The referee on the day was Stanley Rous, who would go on to become FIFA president.

On a fine day, the sun shone on an average-sized Bramall Lane crowd who, given that United had scored 12 goals in their last three home games, and that Burnley had been on the wrong end of an 8-0 drubbing at Anfield on Boxing Day, probably expected to see a few goals. They were not to be disappointed.

Kicking towards the Bramall Lane end, United made all the play from the start and Burnley's defence, which had seen them hold on to their one-goal lead in the cup game, couldn't cope this time around. Very early in the game, Tom Phillipson, playing at inside-right, found himself through on goal only to be brought down in the area, but referee Rous saw nothing wrong with the challenge.

The Blades took only eight minutes to breach the Lancastrian defence, though. Phillipson played a lovely ball to Sid Gibson on the right wing, Johnson met Gibson's cross and, though Burnley keeper Sommerville managed to get a hand to his effort, he could only watch it roll agonisingly over the line.

After 11 minutes, United scored again, Gillespie heading the ball forward for Johnson to latch on to and drive the ball home.

Burnley had a chance to pull one back when Norman Wharton in the United goal spilled the ball into Devine's path, but Len Birks cleared off the line.

Towards the end of the first half, Gillespie rattled the crossbar with a powerful header, then Tunstall felt that he should have had a penalty when fouled in the area, and Phillipson blazed over the bar when it was probably easier to put it on target. At half-time the score was 2-0, but probably should have been more for both teams.

Four minutes after the restart, Johnson completed his 20th hat-trick for the Blades. Gillespie, orchestrating proceedings from inside-left, fed Tunstall, whose perfect cross was headed straight into the net by 'Young' Harry.

In the 61st minute Tunstall himself got in on the scoring action, with a shot from the left that beat the keeper and went just inside the post. He then set up Johnson, who was left with a simple shot to score his fourth.

Birks was called upon again to clear off the line and prevent Burnley from scoring, after Wharton had fumbled, but United seized upon the ball, and, counter-attacking, broke through the middle. Tommy Sampy, running from half-back, was tripped in the area, and, this time, the penalty was given.

Tunstall stepped up to take it, and he scored to put United six up. Only 69 minutes of play had elapsed, and, just two minutes later, it was seven, Gibson's corner from the right being headed home by Phillipson.

Somerville in the Burnley goal was forced to listen to the scoreline being sung to him from the supporters on the Kop, and he was picking the ball out of the net for the eighth time on 80 minutes, Gillespie this time heading home another corner.

Six minutes later, Johnson fed Gibson, running at full speed before slamming the ball home, and United completed the scoring with just three minutes remaining, Phillipson dribbling through the despondent Burnley defence before shooting, slipping on the mud and landing on his back as the ball crossed the line and getting perhaps the biggest roar of the day from the crowd, as double figures were reached.

Johnson had been the star of the show. Three weeks later, he would score four goals again, in a 6-1 win at home to Bury. Although this one would be his last United hat-trick, making 21 in total in league and cup (a Blades record), Johnson would stay at United for another two years, by which point he had scored 201 goals in 313 games, setting United's club goalscoring record.

He moved to Mansfield, and scored over a hundred goals for them. His younger brother, Tommy, would establish himself in the United team of the 1930s, completing four decades of the Johnson family involvement in the club.

Burnley's month would get worse, as they crashed out of the cup at Third Division Swindon Town. They would, however, gain some revenge against United in the next league meeting in the following October, by winning 5-0 at Turf Moor. By the end of the next season, both teams would be involved in a relegation battle that came down to the last match.

v Manchester United 5-1

Football League First Division
3 May 1930
Old Trafford, Manchester
Attendance: 15,268

SHEFFIELD UNITED	MANCHESTER UNITED
Kendall	Steward
Gibson, J.	Jones
Birks	Silcock
Sampy, T.	Bennion
Matthews	Hilditch
Green	Wilson
Gibson, S.	Spence
Pickering	McLenahan
Dunne	Ball
Gillespie	Rowley
Tunstall	McLachlan
Secretary: John Nicholson	Manager: Herbert Bamlett

Supporters of most teams have been through it. A fight against relegation comes down to the last game, nerves are fraught, nails bitten down to the quick, sleepless nights in the days running up to the game. Most Sheffield United fans will immediately recall the games against Chelsea in 1994 or Wigan in 2007, and older fans will forever be scarred by the Walsall game in 1981. In the space of 90 minutes or, in the Chelsea and Walsall games, a handful of minutes, the world collapses around your ears and you are contemplating next season, or perhaps years, in the division below.

The first time that Blades supporters had to endure this final-game worry was 1930. The club had been involved in relegation battles three times previously, but they had always pulled clear with games to spare. Indeed, the fact that they were even involved in a relegation battle in the season was unexpected. On 22 February, after a 3-1 win against Burnley, they were ninth in the table, eight points clear of the relegation places.

There had been a changing of the guard in relation to the goalscoring big-hitters. Harry Johnson, despite three goals in four games at the start of the season, lost his place to Jimmy Dunne, who grasped the nettle by scoring a hat-trick away at Leicester. Dubliner Dunne had been signed in 1926 from Third Division New Brighton, but had been made to bide his time in the reserves while Johnson banged in the goals for the first team.

When he got the opportunity, though, he took his chance, and set a club record for the number of league goals in a season (36). Johnson, meanwhile, would make just four more appearances for the club with a single goal. Still, Billy Gillespie, now 39, and Fred Tunstall, 33, were flying the flag for the 'old guard' in the United forward line.

The week after the Burnley win, the Blades travelled to Roker Park to face relegation-threatened Sunderland. United led 2-1 at half-time and probably should have scored several more as they completely dominated for an hour of the match. They struggled to maintain their high-tempo strategy, and, in a tired last half-hour, they allowed Sunderland to score twice and win the game. It was to be a turning-point for both teams. Sunderland pulled clear of relegation while the Blades won just one of their next ten games, a run which included a 7-5 loss at home to Blackburn, and an 8-1 defeat at Arsenal. With two games remaining for United, the bottom three looked like this, with 21st and 22nd to be relegated in a 42-game season, and two points for a win: 20th Sheffield United P 40 Pts 34 21st. Burnley P 41 Pts 34 22nd Everton P 39 Pts 29.

The fixture list fates had decreed that United had to travel to Everton for their next game. The game echoed the Sunderland match, a 3-2 defeat with United the better side throughout. Everton's winner came in the form of an 87th minute own goal off the unfortunate Tommy Sampy.

Two days later, Everton won at Huddersfield, putting them just a point behind United and Burnley. For the crucial last game, they would be at home to Sunderland, while Burnley entertained second-placed Derby. United, though, had to travel to Old Trafford, so arguably had the most difficult task. A win, though, would guarantee safety due to a superior goal average.

About 1,500 supporters made their way across the Pennines. The team was sent a telegram from their Wednesday counterparts, who were celebrating winning the league title, to wish them luck, and before the game the female Blades in the crowd sang a number from the popular music hall show 'The Bing Boys', which was a United supporter tradition in those days.

One change was made from the team that had lost at Everton. Goalkeeper Wharton, who had shipped six goals in his previous two appearances, made way for Jack Kendall, who had conceded eight against Arsenal in his last game!

After a scrappy start, the 'Laners' (a nickname that has since fallen by the wayside) took the lead. Near the edge of the area, Sid Gibson gave the ball to Dunne, who cleverly beat two defenders. Steward, the Manchester goalkeeper, rushed out to meet him, only for the Blades striker to shoot past him and into the goal.

The United team rushed to hug the Irishman in celebration, but the joy lasted for just five minutes. The ball was lifted into the Blades area and, after a scramble, McLenegan pulled off a superb overhead kick, forcing Kendall to tip the ball over. From the corner, Kendall made a poor clearance with his fist, and Rowley was able to head home.

The Manchester United defence were playing the offside trap brilliantly. On one of the few occasions when the forwards did breach it, midway through the half, Steward was fortunate to save a Dunne effort. Other than that, Tunstall was forced to try his luck from distance, catching the Manchester keeper off his line and forcing him to push the ball away with his face to the goal.

Kendall, too, was tested from distance, but at half-time the scores were level. Meanwhile, both Everton and Burnley were leading their games, meaning that the Blades would have to dig deep in the second half to avoid relegation.

The half very nearly began with a disaster for the Blades. A long ball by Wilson resulted in Len Birks challenging Ball with a dangerous high tackle, which knocked the Manchester player out cold. From the resulting free kick, Wilson's effort beat the unsighted Kendall, only for the ball to crash against the post and out of danger. The Blades were forced to defend more, George Green and Tommy Sampy having to cut out some dangerous attacking, even though their opponents were down to ten men with Ball still missing.

After weathering the third quarter of the game, the Blades pounced on a defensive error to take the lead in the 66th minute. Sid Gibson crossed from the right, and Manchester defender Jones, attempting to make a flying kick, missed the ball and fell flat on his back. The ball landed in the path of Gillespie, who finished perfectly.

Two minutes later there was breathing space for the Blades. Sid Gibson picked the ball up and went on a run down the middle, beating four defenders with lovely control before putting the ball past the keeper, a superb solo goal.

The Blades had the momentum now, Tunstall putting an opportunistic long shot just wide, and shortly after, latching on to a pass from Gillespie in the area. In challenging him, Silcock handled the ball, and the referee awarded a penalty. Tunstall stepped up to take the kick, and he put an unstoppable shot into the net; 73 minutes gone, 4-1.

The home team tried in vain to put attacks together, but the Blades' backs were equal to the task, as their forwards pressed for a fifth. It came rather fortunately. Gillespie challenged the keeper for a Sid Gibson cross from the goal line, the keeper got hold of the ball, but fumbled and it dropped over the line. Gillespie was credited with the goal, but contemporary reports describe it as a Steward own goal.

Four goals in 11 minutes had turned the game on its head, and of the five that the team had scored, Sid Gibson had been involved in four. His distribution and crossing had been of top quality throughout the game. He had received a lot of criticism since the Blades paid a club-record £5,000 for him from Nottingham Forest the previous season, seemingly being low on both fitness and confidence. His performance against Manchester United was considered his best in his spell at the club, but what a time to turn it on!

Sheffield United had won 5-1, which meant that they were safe regardless of other results. Wilson's effort against the post had, perhaps, been the crucial moment, and had the result gone another way, they would have been relegated, as Burnley had won 6-2 and Everton 4-1. As it was, they secured a place in the First Division that they had already held for 37 years, although they would finally succumb to relegation four years later. The club would be involved in many more last-day dramas as the years rolled by, but those 11 minutes at Old Trafford would live long in the memory for those who were there.

v Leeds United 3-1

FA Cup Fifth Round
15 February 1936
Bramall Lane
Attendance: 68,287

SHEFFIELD UNITED	LEEDS UNITED
Smith	McInroy
Hooper	Sproston
Wilkinson	Milburn
Jackson	Edwards
Johnson	McDougall
McPherson	Browne
Barton	Armes
Barclay	Brown
Dodds	Kelly
Pickering	Furness
Williams	Cochrane
Secretary Manager: Teddy Davison	Manager: Billy Hampson

These days, cup ties tend to draw smaller crowds than league games, especially in the early rounds, unless clubs are drawn against 'big-name' teams. This was not always the case though. In the pre-Premier League era, the FA Cup was the ultimate, and certainly the most romantic, domestic prize, and cup games tended to draw the more casual supporter through the turnstiles. Three times in their history, United were able to attract crowds of over 60,000 to Bramall Lane, and these were all for cup games.

In 1926, with the Blades as cup holders, 62,041 watched a fourth-round defeat to Sunderland, and in 1939, a fifth-round tie against, of all teams, Grimsby Town, attracted 62,022 spectators for a goalless draw. Sandwiched between these is the record attendance for a game at Bramall Lane, against Leeds United in the fifth round of the 1936 FA Cup.

The club's proud record of 41 consecutive years in the top flight had ended in 1934, and top scorer Jimmy Dunne had moved on to Arsenal. Attendances dropped, and on only one occasion in the first season back in the second tier did more than 25,000 turn up to Bramall Lane, and that for a Boxing Day local derby match against Barnsley. Any hopes of an immediate return to the top flight in 1934/35 were over by Christmas, in fact relegation looked like an outside possibility, the only bright point being the emergence of teenage forward 'Jock' Dodds, who scored 19 goals in 28 starts for the team. He continued this form into the 1935/36 season, but the team were still inconsistent and struggled to keep pace with the promotion-chasing pack.

On 21 December, a 7-0 win over Hull City (in front of just 10,413 at the Lane) sparked a run of form in all competitions, putting them in promotion contention and also on a run in the FA Cup. Scoring a hat-trick in the Hull game was Jack Pickering, the oldest serving member of the team, now in his 11th season. The cup run had begun at Turf Moor, against fellow Second Division team Burnley, with a 0-0 draw, the Blades winning the replay 2-1. They were rewarded with another trip to Lancashire, against Preston this time. Again, a 0-0 draw, and a win in a replay at Bramall Lane.

The fifth-round draw pitted United against Yorkshire rivals Leeds United, a club less than two decades old. A previous Leeds club, Leeds City, has been disbanded by the Football League due to illegal payments. Now in the top flight, Leeds had escaped relegation in 1935 and, at the time of meeting United in the cup, were relatively safe in mid-table. They possessed one of the finest attacking wing-halves in the country in England player Willie Edwards, who had been at Leeds as long as Pickering had been at the Blades.

The tie, then, was an attractive one for Yorkshire football fans, an in-form Second Division Blades team against a top-flight Leeds team who had never made it to a quarter-final before. In spite of a miserable grey and misty day, the crowds poured in from all corners of the West Riding (South Yorkshire would not come into being for another 38 years so Leeds and Sheffield were still in the same 'riding'), and took up any spot possible. The sacred turf of the cricket pitch was covered with a mass of people, and a number of them clung to the cricket scoreboard to see above the masses. The mist was brightened by red berets of the United female faithful. By 1:30, the turnstiles were closed, while police horses were employed to keep the touchlines clear of people, and to allow the players on to the field. Sadly, there were almost 300 injuries of varying degrees of severity, and worse still, two eventual deaths after the game. Those with higher vantage points were put to work by those without, to replay impromptu commentaries of the game, which almost became secondary to the happenings within the massive crowd.

Leeds started the brighter of the two teams, well organised and playing crisp, passing football. After 14 minutes, they were awarded a corner, and Furness was left unmarked to score a free header.

Their lead lasted for just three minutes, though, as the Blades' Harold Barton, a winger signed from Liverpool the previous season, had the beating of Milburn on the right due to sheer speed. His cross glanced back off Dodds's head, and it fell to Pickering who shot home.

Tom Johnson made a couple of crucial challenges to stop Kelly running down the middle. (Johnson was the son of 'Old' Harry and brother of United's record goalscorer 'Young' Harry, and had established himself as a regular starter at half-back). On a third occasion, though, Kelly beat him and was through on goal. He shot, but keeper Jack 'Smiler' Smith pulled off a fine save to deny him. The Blades then had more chances before half-time, Dodds heading wide twice, before the referee blew for the interval. With the fog, crowd issues and fading light, the referee wisely decided to reduce the break by five minutes. The game resumed with intensity, and at one point Harry Hooper charged Milburn, so the two decided to settle the matter with a spell of wrestling on the ground before being separated.

In the 55th minute Bobby Barclay, United's clever inside-forward, played the ball to Bert Williams on the left, who put a lovely ball into the box. Dodds beat McInroy, the Leeds keeper, to the ball and was able to put United 2-1 up.

At the other end, Brown was put clean through, Johnson bringing him down from behind in the area with a last-ditch challenge. It should have been a penalty, but the referee waved away the Leeds appeals.

Barton and Barclay were tormenting the Leeds players on the right side of the pitch, especially when Dodds ventured to the right to join them, and it was Barclay who was able to feed Pickering, who switched the ball on to his left foot and into the goal at the Bramall Lane end of the ground. The fog and light were so bad, and views so restricted by the mass of people, that few on the Shoreham Street

Kop saw the goal go in, and only knew the score was 3-1 from the noise emanating from the opposite end.

The Blades were through to the quarter-finals, and they were now 15 games without a defeat since the Hull win in December. By the time they faced fellow promotion contenders Spurs in the next round, they were top of the league, and ran out 3-1 winners at Bramall Lane. Another Second Division London team, Fulham, were beaten in the semi-final, 2-1 at Molineux. This was the last of a record 22-game unbeaten run, as Fulham took some revenge in the following game by winning 1-0 at the Lane in the league. In the cup final, United faced Arsenal, and lost to a single goal scored by Ted Drake. It was to be the club's last cup final appearance to date. Unfortunately, only three league games were won from the last eight after the Fulham semi-final, and United missed out on promotion by three points.

The remarkable crowd of 15 February 1936 remains as United's record attendance, and is very unlikely ever to be bettered.

v Tottenham Hotspur **6-1**

Football League Second Division
6 May 1939
Bramall Lane
Attendance: 38,460

SHEFFIELD UNITED	TOTTENHAM HOTSPUR
Smith	Hooper
Cox	Ward
Carr	Nicholson
Eggleston	Burgess
Johnson	Hitchins
Settle	Buckingham
Pickering	Hall
Hampson	Duncan
Henson	Cox
Hagan	Ludford
Reid	Miller
Secretary Manager: Teddy Davison	Manager: Peter McWilliam

Following a first-ever relegation in 1933/34, the Blades challenged twice for promotion in the following three seasons, but they fell short both times. In 1935/36, despite a record-breaking 22-game unbeaten run, the exertions of a run to the cup final cost them, and, in 1937/38, a last-day defeat meant that they finished level with Manchester United on points, but the Blades lost out on goal average.

Across Sheffield, Wednesday, meanwhile, had started the decade as league champions, and had finished in the top three on three occasions in the early 1930s, but they had also been relegated in 1937. Sheffield, for the first time since 1892, had no top-flight representation. In fact, Wednesday had very nearly made it back-to-back relegations, a win away at Spurs in the last game saving them from a drop to the Third Division in 1937/38.

To boost the side that had so nearly won promotion, United had signed a young inside-forward from Derby by the name of Jimmy Hagan. Derby had wanted £3,000 for him, but the Blades board had not wanted to pay that amount. After negotiation, they got him for £75 under the asking price. You wouldn't want the United leadership of that era (or most eras, to be honest) negotiating for your life!

Sheffield United Greatest Games

As 1938/39 coincided with United's 40th anniversary, there was a strong desire for the team to win promotion to mark the occasion. Fittingly, they were captained by a Sheffield-born player with strong family connections going back almost to the beginning of United's history, Tom Johnson. The team made a steady, but not particularly impressive, start to the campaign, and supporter confidence was dealt a huge blow when Jock Dodds, the top goalscorer, was sold to Blackpool for £10,000 after handing in a transfer request for 'family reasons'. There were injury problems too. In January and February three first-team regulars were ruled out for the vast majority of the rest of the season, including Jack Pickering, now in his 12th year at the club.

Away form was good, and, although it was not until the game against Luton in late January that a team scored more than one goal against them at home, there were as many draws at Bramall Lane in the season as there were wins. In those days of two points for a win, these single points collected by United kept them in contention, as did a run of eight games without defeat from the end of March and encompassing all of April. At the beginning of March, though, a Sheffield derby had been lost 1-0 at Hillsborough, albeit through a 'gift' of a goal.

Wednesday were in the middle of a run of results which had lifted them from mid-table since the New Year. They finished their season a week before United, with a 1-0 win over Spurs at Hillsborough. This put them in second place, a point ahead of the Blades but with an inferior goal average. What it meant was that one of the Sheffield clubs would be back in the First Division for the 1939/40 season, it was now in United's hands to decide which one it would be.

A win or a draw at home to Spurs would mean that United would be promoted at the expense of their city neighbours, although an unlikely 7-7 draw would have tipped the goal average advantage to the Owls. On a sunny May day, 38,460 supporters, of both Sheffield persuasions and including the entire Wednesday team, made their way to Bramall Lane to see which way the pendulum would swing. Jack Pickering made just his second start since his injury, coming in for the injured Barton, otherwise the team was essentially the one that had been unbeaten for the prior eight matches.

Spurs kicked off, towards the Bramall Lane end with the sun in their eyes. United got possession immediately, and a punt forward was chested down by Bobby Reid, who put in a wonderful pass to find Jimmy Hagan on the right. Hagan dribbled down the wing, and crossed low. George Henson dummied as Harry Hampson, running at full speed, met the ball from five yards out, shooting home.

From Spurs kicking off to Hampson scoring had taken just ten seconds. Not the start the Wednesday Hotspur supporters in the crowd had hoped for!

Spurs came back at United. Ludford met a Cox cross, forcing Jack Smith to parry and a United defender was able to clear.

After ten minutes, Pickering played in Henson, whose cross was met by Hagan. As the Spurs keeper came out to meet him, Hagan slotted a low shot with pace past him and into the goal; 2-0.

United's Bobby Reid, a Scottish winger signed from Brentford earlier in the season, was causing Cox problems down the left, and at one point Reid even balanced the ball on his head as he moved forward. On the opposite wing, Pickering, without the match fitness of the rest of the team, was less of a threat, although he was still able to play some lethal balls.

Hall caused United keeper Smith a moment of concern with a swerving shot that he needed two attempts to hold on to, then, at the other end, Hampson caused Hooper to save from a headed attempt. Reid again marauded down the left, crossing for Hagan, only to see the shot go over the bar, then Spurs had another good chance, Ludford's shot causing Smith to parry before grabbing the ball at the second attempt. In the 35th minute, a long ball up the middle was controlled by Henson, who ran with it, easily fending off the challenge of Hitchins before finding himself with room to shoot from about 15 yards, his shot beating Hooper to put United 3-0 up with 35 minutes gone.

Six minutes later, and it was four. Reid again came down the left and put in a great cross, Hagan again running on to the ball, beating his man and finishing neatly. Half-time came, and United's promotion looked more than secure. Even the most optimistic of the Wednesday contingent knew that United, barring a disaster, would not concede five second half goals, and the Blades fans were in jubilant mood.

Just after half-time, play was stopped as the referee had mud in his eye, Hagan helping him to remove it, but this good turn was not rewarded moments later when Hagan felt he was fouled in the box, only for the referee to wave away the protests. Thanks for nothing, ref!

The second half was, perhaps understandably, less frenetic than the first, although Reid, and the victim of his tormenting, Cox, were both booked after a brief skirmish. United had taken their foot off the gas a little, and Spurs were able to take advantage of this after 64 minutes. Cox's cross was met by Ludford in the middle, whose shot was parried by Smith only to land at the feet of Miller. With Smith still on the deck, Miller blasted the ball, which hit the underside of the bar and bounced over the line. After a brief consultation between referee and linesman, the goal was given.

The goal woke United up again, some fine interplay between Reid and Hagan giving the latter the chance to shoot with power. Hooper saved, but could not hold on. The ball rebounded back off Hagan and straight up into the air. Bill Nicholson attempted to clear with his head, but only as far as Henson, running in from deep, who was able to drive the ball home. Nicholson, incidentally, would later manage Spurs to the first league and cup double of the century in 1960/61. Three years after the game at Bramall Lane, he was quoted as saying that he was 'still dizzy' from trying to mark Hagan in this match!

Hagan completed his hat-trick with 15 minutes remaining with a clever piece of trickery, feigning a pass to Henson and wrong-footing the defenders, creating a simple finish for himself.

Spurs were well beaten now, and both Hagan and Arthur Eggleston had chances saved by Hooper as the game drew to a close. As the whistle sounded, supporters invaded the pitch to celebrate, and congregated in front of the directors' box where the players re-appeared to receive the adulation of the crowd.

The team made a strong start to life back in the top flight after the summer break, winning two and drawing one of the first three games, and were sitting in second place after beating Leeds at Elland Road on 2 September. The previous day, though, Hitler's Germany had invaded Poland, and, understandably, football was not high on the list of public priorities. Less than 10,000 had turned up for the

Leeds game. Within 24 hours of the match, war had been declared. League football was suspended immediately, and it remained so for seven years. United would have to wait to reap the benefits of the hammering of Tottenham.

v Bradford (Park Avenue) 4-0

Football League North
19 April 1946
Park Avenue, Bradford
Attendance: 18,841

SHEFFIELD UNITED	BRADFORD PARK AVENUE
Smith	Parr
Furniss	Steven
Shimwell	Hepworth
Machent	White
Latham	Danskin
Forbes	Greenwood
Rickett	Smith
Nightingale	Shackleton
Thomson, C.	Gibbons
Hagan	Downie
Pickering	Walker
Secretary Manager: Teddy Davison	Manager: Fred Emery

Although the Second World War ended in 1945, victory against Japan did not come until August, and there were still thousands of Allied troops still stationed overseas into and beyond the following year. Because of this, normal football service was not resumed until the 1946/47 season.

The competition that was set up in its place, though, was a vast improvement on the fare that had been served during the previous six seasons.

Two divisions, split geographically, were created from the First and Second Division teams of the aborted 1939/40 season, and line-ups began to become more consistent, with less reliance on 'guest' players from other clubs as had been the case. The FA Cup also resumed with, for the only time, two-legged ties.

Life in the Football League North started badly for United, losing 6-0 at St James' Park in the first match, then, even worse, losing twice in seven days to Wednesday. Gradually, though, they began to field a settled team, a mixture of older, pre-war players and young players who had taken their chances in the war years when the older players were away with the armed forces. Furniss, Latham, Forbes, Brook and Nightingale in particular would be regular features for the rest of the 1940s.

Following the inauspicious start to the season, United then went on to win 23 of their next 31 fixtures, and they had hit a 100 goals tally by the 35th game.

A 4-3 aggregate defeat to Stoke in the FA Cup was followed by a run of 12 games without loss, ten of them being wins, and United headed into a busy Easter weekend of three games in four days. Remarkably, given this run, Everton were still in touch with the Blades, just two points behind them as United travelled to Park Avenue for the Good Friday game. Bradford Park Avenue were almost a permanent fixture in the second tier before the war and were arguably Bradford's bigger club, while City were languishing in the Third Division. Unusually, for two teams in the same city, they played in the same colours as their neighbours.

If United were strong favourites going into the game, Bradford's hopes were further dented with an early injury to young amateur midfielder White after just five minutes of the kick-off, after one of his own players stood on his foot! Bradford did well, in fact, to keep the score goalless until half-time, although the Blades were almost falling over each other in the box, they were attacking with so many players!

After 47 minutes, Albert Nightingale beat Hepworth and sent a low, hard shot into the bottom corner. It was Nightingale's 20th goal of the season, and an opening goal which saw the floodgates open.

Next up was Walter Rickett, cutting in from the right wing to run through a crowd of three Bradford defenders, and firing low past the keeper.

The third goal came after a Bobby Reid shot was blocked, falling to Charlie Thompson, who had an empty goal at his mercy.

Thompson was a player who had seemed destined for great things, but he had broken his leg two seasons earlier and had never really regained his pace.

The final goal came from the great Jimmy Hagan, who had only returned from war duties the previous month, as he hit a shot from just outside the area which glanced off the underside of the crossbar and bounced into the net.

The game finished 4-0, while Everton lost 2-0 at Barnsley, which meant United were four points clear. Although there were still four games to go, a great second half had put the Blades in command of the league.

On the Easter Saturday, 36,079 turned up to Bramall Lane for the game against Manchester City, hoping to see United at least maintain the gap, but the team were 2-0 down at half-time and lost 3-2, while Everton won.

They were to be the last points that Everton would pick up, though. They lost their last three games and United were confirmed champions the following Saturday, despite another defeat to Manchester City, this time at Maine Road.

Because it was not the official resumption of the league, it is a championship that has been largely forgotten, even though the FA Cup winners that year, Derby, do count as official winners, so football was definitely being taken seriously.

To paint a picture of the strength of the Football League North compared to its southern counterpart, the champions of that competition were Birmingham City, who failed to gain promotion from the Second Division the following season. Meanwhile, five of top six of the First Division in 1946/47 had been in the North section (United being one of them).

United had won the strongest league in England, and this is something that should, within the club if nowhere else, be remembered and celebrated more than it has been.

v Sheffield Wednesday 7-3

18

Football League Second Division
8 September 1951
Bramall Lane
Attendance: 51,075

SHEFFIELD UNITED	SHEFFIELD WEDNESDAY
Burgin	McIntosh
Furniss	Jackson
Cox	Kenny
Hitchen	Gannon
Latham	Turton
Shaw, J.	Witcomb
Ringstead	Finney
Smith, F. A.	Sewell
Brook	Woodhead
Hagan	Thomas
Hawksworth	Rickett
Secretary Manager: Teddy Davison	Manager: Eric Taylor

Following the Second World War, United had made a strong start back in football. After winning the Football League North, they finished sixth in their first season back in the First Division. Within three years, though, they had been relegated, a lack of squad strength costing them their place in the English football elite. A year on from this relegation, both Sheffield clubs were in the running for promotion from the Second Division. Wednesday gained revenge for the 1938/39 season by pipping United to promotion on goal average with a last-day draw against Spurs, but they came straight back down the following season, and the two teams were back for a fourth season together in Second Division.

United supporters had not been particularly confident in their prospects for the 1951/52 season after a disappointing mid-table finish in the previous campaign, and the only strengthening from the transfer market was the signing of 'Little' Fred Smith (one of two Fred Smiths playing for United at the time), a forward from Hull. They did, of course, have the magic of Jimmy Hagan to call upon, ably supported by the wingers, Alf Ringstead and Derek Hawksworth, who had joined during the previous season. Hagan could, though, so easily have been lining up for Wednesday, as they had attempted to sign him for £32,500, which would have been a

British record transfer fee, but Hagan, to his credit, turned down the Owls.

By the time the teams met at Bramall Lane on the second Saturday in September, both teams were in the top three, on the same points, and the Sheffield derby was, if possible, more eagerly anticipated than usual. United had scored 17 goals in their first five games so were in a rich vein of goalscoring form.

Wednesday kicked off towards the Bramall Lane end and went straight on to the attack. Former Blade Walter Rickett, who had joined the Owls from Blackpool, crossed, and Ted Burgin in the United goal was forced to fist it away and out for a throw-in. The ball was played back into the middle, Thomas connecting with it and beating Burgin with a rising shot just inside the post. Wednesday were a goal up with just 90 seconds on the clock.

United fought back. In the tenth minute the ball was played through to Ringstead, who had space to shoot. His effort beat the Wednesday keeper McIntosh, and, although Jackson cleared from the goalmouth, the ball had crossed the line. Had it not, a United forward followed up anyway, but the goal was credited to Ringstead; 1-1.

United won six corners in the first 15 minutes, and the sixth almost resulted in a goal, McIntosh just clawing the ball away. Shortly after this, at the other end, Fred Furniss had to clear off the line from a Woodhead shot.

Harry Hitchen, bringing the ball out of defence, took on and beat two defenders and found Harold Brook on the right-hand corner of the area. Brook turned and hit a shot which swerved and gave McIntosh no chance. Afer 17 minutes the Blades were in the lead. Later in the half, Fred Smith won a penalty for United, tripped in the area by Kenny. Furniss took the spot-kick well, but McIntosh pulled off an impressive one-handed save and was able to recover and clear the ball. Half-time arrived with the score 2-1 to United.

The second half started with the same intensity as the first, both teams creating chances. Woodhead shot over the bar, McIntosh was forced to tip over when Turton nearly turned the ball into his own net and a Hitchen effort hit the side netting, causing half of the ground to celebrate what they thought was a goal.

On the hour mark, Woodhead brought the game level again, with an effort from the corner of the area, and he almost made it three for the Owls when his shot was touched by Burgin on to the inside of the post, only to bounce straight back to the keeper.

Hagan headed over from a corner, and the next significant attack, with 67 minutes on the clock, resulted in an almighty scramble in the Wednesday area. Hagan shot first, then Smith, then Ringstead, the ball being blocked by defenders and, in one case, the post, before Brook's shot went into the goal, McIntosh unable to stop it as he was being hampered by one of his own defenders. Five minutes later United doubled their lead. A Brook pass found Hawksworth unmarked on the left of the area, and he placed the ball into the bottom corner.

Ringstead then got a stroke of luck, in the 74th minute, his shot being saved by McIntosh but rebounding off Turton into the goal; 5-2.

United attacked again, Hawksworth hugging the left touchline before putting a cross in for Smith to head home. United had scored four goals in 11 minutes.

Wednesday now rallied, and they pulled one back with three minutes left to play. Although Cox claimed to have cleared Thomas's shot off the line, the linesman adjudged it to have crossed, and a goal was awarded.

United were not finished though, and Brook put a low shot past McIntosh in the 89th minute to make it 7-3.

The victory put United top of the table. The following Saturday, United treated the Bramall Lane faithful to another goal-fest, beating West Ham 6-1, and by the end of October were four points clear at the top. Only eight wins were gained from the next 28 games, though, and, even though one of these wins was a 3-1 win at Hillsborough to complete a Sheffield 'double' (they would also beat them by the same 3-1 scoreline in front of 20,000 in a County Cup semi-final to make it a unique 'treble'), it was Wednesday who would go on to win the Second Division championship, as a young forward by the name of Derek Dooley emerged from the reserves to score 46 goals in the season, a Wednesday record.

United, meanwhile, finished in a disappointing 11th, causing manager Teddy Davison to resign after two decades in charge. The 7-3 win, though, would be remembered by Blades fans for many years to follow, and the events of the following season would soon erase the disappointment.

v West Ham United 3-1

Football League Second Division
18 April 1953
Bramall Lane
Attendance: 32,403

SHEFFIELD UNITED	WEST HAM UNITED
Burgin	Gregory
Furniss	Wright
Shaw, G.	Cantwell
Shaw, J.	Parker
Latham	Allison
Toner	Bing
Ringstead	Southren
Hagan	Barratt
Browning	Dixon
Brook	Gazzard
Hawksworth	Hooper
Manager: Reg Freeman	Manager: Ted Fenton

The year 1952 was the end of an era at Sheffield United Football Club, as secretary-manager Teddy Davidson stepped down after 20 years in charge. United looked to near-neighbours Rotherham for his replacement.

Reg Freeman had won promotion to the Second Division for the first time in the Millers' history, having narrowly missed out in three of the previous four seasons, and the Blades board felt that he was the man to bring the club back into the English football elite.

Freeman was promised no interference in team selection, but he chose not to make any new signings anyway. The team had scored 90 goals in the previous season, but had conceded 76, so Freeman promoted Graham Shaw and Howard Johnson from the reserves to bolster the defence.

The plan worked, although Johnson would only play 15 games before breaking a collarbone and allowing Harold Latham, the giant 'Old Chainhorse' to win back his place.

The board's trust in Freeman was well rewarded. Despite losing two of the opening five games, they were top of the league by the end of November and stayed there for the rest of the campaign, demolishing Lincoln 6-1, Bury 4-0, Leicester 7-2, Swansea 7-1, and Plymouth 5-0 on the way.

Freeman was able to field a consistent side, and five players made double-figure scoring tallies. Alf Ringstead led the way with 22, followed by Harold Brook, Len Browning and Jimmy Hagan (now 35 years old) all on 17 and Derek Hawksworth on ten.

Going into the West Ham game in April, the Blades were six points clear of third-placed Luton Town. A United win would clinch promotion if Luton failed to win at Everton. The Hammers were a perennial mid-table Second Division club at the time, having been in the division for 21 years.

On a sunny April day the teams took to the field and the Blades started brightly, winning four corners to the Hammers' one in the opening exchanges. From two of these corners, both taken by Ringstead, Gregory was forced to save from headers, first from Hagan, then from Brook. Next, from a free kick, Hagan chipped the ball over the wall, but Ringstead, turning 180 degrees, could only head wide.

There was a level of anxiety and desperation in United's play, particularly in the forward line, where simple passes were going to defenders, and they were almost made to pay for this when Harry Hooper, son of former Blade Harry senior, found himself clean through. Ted Burgin, the United keeper, hesitated, allowing Hooper to shoot past him, only to see his shot hit the side netting. United then went close. Bill Toner, running in from midfield with the ball, managed to get a shot on target, only for it to hit Brook on the way through and deflect off the post.

In the 42nd minute, the opening goal of the game came, albeit a little fortunately, Brook and Ringstead playing a one-two and Brook scuffing a shot which hit the inside of the post before going in.

Half-time came, and with United leading 1-0, the manually updated scoreboard showed that the scores were level at Goodison Park 1-1. This allowed United to start the second half with less anxiety, and they could have added to their tally in the early exchanges of the half, the West Ham goalkeeper having to deal with shots from Brook and Hawksworth.

The pressure was now becoming relentless from the men in red and white. Gregory was forced to tip a Brook effort around the post, and Hagan shot just over from 20 yards. Hagan then put in a wonderful pass to Browning, who, after one touch, blasted the ball into the roof of the net to put United 2-0 up after 57 minutes.

Still the Blades came forward. Hawksworth crossed from the left, but Ringstead headed over, then left-back Graham Shaw got in on the action, dribbling the ball inside from the wing, beating two men as he did so, only for his shot to zip across the goalmouth.

United could have racked up another huge score in a season full of them, but found their lead reduced to one in the 79th minute, albeit all down to their own making. A loose back-pass from Toner to Burgin was picked up by Dixon and, with Burgin out of position, Dixon was able to slot home, even though he was virtually on the touchline by the time he had picked up the loose ball.

The nerves returned to the team and the crowd, and the Hammers tried to use this to their advantage. Barrett should have done better with a chance that he put wide. Southren then put a shot in from the right wing into the side netting.

United, though, settled the game, the collective nerves and the small matter of promotion with three minutes to go, Browning crossing for Brook to put a looping header over the keeper and into the goal.

United had won, and the news came through that there had been no change to the scoreline at Everton. The promotion celebrations could begin.

While United had been beating West Ham, Wednesday, struggling in the top flight, had gone from a half-time 3-1 lead at Villa Park to lose the game 4-3, and looked in real danger. The following Saturday, though, they beat Sunderland 4-0 at Hillsborough and were safe. Sheffield had two teams together in the top flight for the first time in 20 years.

United, meanwhile, travelled to Craven Cottage, knowing that a win would make them Second Division champions. Despite dominating the game, they had to come back from a goal down to win the game in the 88th minute when Browning, who had levelled the game, played a ball through to Brook to score. The Second Division trophy, won by Wednesday the year before, would stay in the city.

Freeman's thoughts turned to life in the First Division. 'I will be satisfied,' he said 'to hold our own for the first season or two.'

Sheffield United 3 West Ham United 1

Sadly, though, while he would keep the team in the top division, he would only be in charge for two more seasons after the promotion, as he was taken suddenly ill and died in August 1955. His record was as a United manager who won the Second Division championship in his first season at the club and kept the club in the top flight.

v Tottenham Hotspur 3-0

20 FA Cup Fourth Round
25 January 1958
White Hart Lane, London
Attendance: 51,136

SHEFFIELD UNITED	TOTTENHAM HOTSPUR
Hodgkinson	Ditchburn
Coldwell	Hills
Shaw, G.	Hopkins
Richardson	Blanchflower
Shaw, J.	Norman
Summers	Ryden
Lewis	Medwin
Russell	Harmer
Pace	Smith
Hawksworth	Brooks
Hodgson	Dyson
Manager: Joe Mercer	Manager: Jimmy Anderson

Joe Mercer had been a highly rated defender for Everton and Arsenal, and had played for England on 31 occasions in full and wartime internationals. In 1954, while playing for Arsenal against Liverpool at 39 years old, he broke his leg and was forced to retire the following year. After the sudden death of Blades' boss Reg Freeman shortly before the start of the 1955/56 season, United approached Mercer to take over as manager.

Unfortunately, the season, blighted by injuries, saw the club relegated, and a poor run of results in December and January of 1956/57 meant that the club were out of the promotion picture come the end of the season. The board kept faith with Mercer, and he was responsible for building a famous defence (the 'WM' strategy yet to give way to the 4-4-2) that would play consistently together until 1964 – Alan Hodgkinson in goal, Cec Coldwell and Graham Shaw as backs, Joe Shaw at centre-half with Brian Richardson and Gerry Summers as half-backs. Of the six, only Summers had come from outside of the club youth setup.

The start of the 1957/58 season was a disappointment mainly due to a lack of goals scored. By Christmas Day, when the team lost 1-0 away at Blackburn, only three teams had scored fewer than United. Mercer turned to the transfer market, paying £12,000 for

Sheffield United 3 Tottenham Hotspur 0

Aston Villa's forward Derek Pace. Pace scored after eight minutes of his Boxing Day debut, as United beat Blackburn 4-2. Also scoring in the game was 17-year-old Kevin Lewis, in just his second game.

Mercer's team scored 15 goals in 4 games, including a 5-1 demolition of Grimsby Town in the cup (Lewis getting two), which set up a trip to top-flight Tottenham Hotspur.

Having built a team around midfielder Danny Blanchflower, Spurs, runners-up in the First Division the previous season, had thrashed fellow First Division side Leicester 4-0 at White Hart Lane in the third round. Very few people gave the Blades much of a chance of getting anything from the game, even if their form had improved since the arrival of Pace.

Thousands made the journey from Sheffield to North London on a cold, snowy day, and were rewarded for their efforts within just two minutes as United took a surprise lead. Graham Shaw played the ball into the goalmouth, Richardson flicked the ball on to Derek Hawksworth, who headed it down into the path of Pace. Pace, eight yards out, put a low shot past Ditchburn in the Tottenham goal. Ditchburn would confess that it was an error on his part. 'I should have got down in time to stop that one,' he said, but, regardless, United were a goal up.

Mercer had devised a plan to contain Spurs, which involved Billy Hodgson, playing at inside-forward, sticking to Blanchflower like glue whenever Tottenham had the ball, preventing him from his usual orchestration of play from the middle of the park. When United had the ball, they were to play triangles around Blanchflower so that he was unable to win the ball back for his team.

The conditions were also playing a part. A layer of snow on the ground meant that players often lost their footing, but United adapted better than their London opponents, using longer passes while Spurs struggled to change from their short-passing game.

In the eighth minute, Hills, the Spurs right-back, thought the ball had gone out for a throw-in, probably correctly, and picked it up. The referee and linesman, though, felt that it had not fully crossed the line, and awarded a free kick for handball. Graham Shaw put the free kick into the box and Billy Russell grazed it with his head and into the net.

United were two ahead.

Sheffield United Greatest Games

Spurs now found United difficult to break down, with defenders all putting in great tackles. On the one occasion they did break through, Hodgkinson was equal to Smith's effort, then Hawksworth had two shots saved by Ditchburn at the other end. Shortly before half-time, Spurs registered only their second shot on target, this time from Dyson, again saved by Hodgkinson.

Early in the second half, Pace had the chance to score United's third, after jockeying Norman and getting past him, but his shot was straight at the keeper.

Hodgkinson required treatment after taking a knock while collecting the ball from Smith's feet, and he was called into further action as Spurs tried to make some impact on the game, learning from United's approach by abandoning their passing game and punting the ball long. Hodgkinson was kept busy with saves against both Medwin and Dyson in quick succession, and the wall stopped a Smith effort from a free kick.

Any hopes of Tottenham rescuing anything from the game were ended in the 83rd minute, with the best goal of the game. Derek Hawksworth latched on to a pass from Lewis, and, 20 yards out on the left, shot across the goalkeeper and into the bottom right-hand corner, sending the travelling Unitedites into raptures. Spurs were a beaten team now, and United won two corners before the final whistle completed a famous cup shock.

Only five First Division clubs remained in the cup by the fifth round, leading one journalist to moan about the top players being 'pampered these days' and therefore not up to the fight in 'David and Goliath' games, and worrying about the 'big business' approach of the league and the top clubs. The more things change, the more they stay the same!

United's reward for the beating of Spurs was a home tie against a West Brom team which included Don Howe and Bobby Robson in the line-up and were challenging at the top of the First Division.

A crowd of 54,150 turned up to Bramall Lane for the West Brom game, which was the highest crowd at the ground since the war and would only be bettered once afterwards. West Brom took an early lead, but Lewis levelled in the 77th minute to take the game to a replay. As Wednesday's tie at Old Trafford had been postponed, the draw came out as Sheffield United or West Brom v Manchester

United or Sheffield Wednesday, an outside chance of an all-Sheffield quarter-final at Bramall Lane.

Albion, though, were vastly superior in the replay, winning 4-1 (and even the one United goal was an own goal) while the Owls lost 3-0.

Although United won 11 of their remaining 14 games in the league after the cup exit, the gap from the first half of the season was too wide to bridge. Although Mercer's team had begun to click, he would be tempted away by a bigger club when Villa came knocking the following December, and would go on to great success in the next decade, winning the league, FA Cup and Cup-Winners' Cup with Manchester City.

With the famous defence, and with Pace and Lewis up front, Mercer had laid the foundations on which the popular Sheffield United team of the 1960s would be built. The Spurs game had given some notice of things to come.

v Newcastle United 3-1

21

FA Cup Quarter-Final
4 March 1961
St James' Park, Newcastle
Attendance: 54,640

SHEFFIELD UNITED	NEWCASTLE UNITED
Hodgkinson	Mitchell
Coldwell	McKinney
Shaw, G.	McMichael
Richardson	Neale
Shaw, J.	Thompson
Summers	Bell
Hodgson	Hughes
Russell	Allchurch
Pace	White
Kettleborough	McGuigan
Simpson	Scanlan
Manager: John Harris	Manager: Charlie Mitten

Sticking with essentially the same squad that Joe Mercer had put together paid off immediately for his successor, John Harris, in his second full season in charge. As 1961 began, they were top of the Second Division and that famous, consistent line-up at the back, were the foundations of this success, proving to be the best defence in the division.

Up front, Derek 'Doc' Pace was banging in the goals, having scored 21 in 32 league games by the end of February. Although they had lost to Third Division Bury in their first-ever League Cup tie, the team had put together an FA Cup run which had seen them make it to the quarter-finals.

Strangely, given that Pace was in scoring form in the league, he had not scored in the cup run, and scoring duties in the competition seemed to have been left to Billy Russell. Russell had been a Mercer signing in 1957, spotted by him playing as an amateur for Rhyl, for £1,000 (plus two friendlies at Rhyl over the next two years).

A fast, right-footed player, Russell was equally at home on the wing or in the middle, but he had missed most of the 1959/60 season after breaking his leg away to Bristol Rovers. Back fit for the new season, he had scored 11 league goals by the time United began the cup campaign on the first Saturday in January.

The third-round draw had given United a tough trip to Goodison Park, against an Everton team sitting fifth in the top flight, but the Blades pulled off a shock 1-0 win, with Russell scoring in the first half. He followed this goal up with two more against the Second Division's bottom club, Lincoln in the next round, then another against First Division Blackburn, both at Bramall Lane, to put United through to the quarter-finals.

Again, the draw pitted them against First Division opponents, this time relegation-threatened Newcastle. In spite of the Blades' form in both competitions, Newcastle were favourites to progress. They had finished eighth in the previous season, and they boasted one of the best attacks in the country, led by top scorer Len White. They also, though, had the worst defence in the top league, and this had them in real trouble (they had conceded 87 in 31 by the time of the quarter-final, ten more than any other team in the division).

The Blades created a shock before the game even began. In an age before ever-changing replica away strips, clubs only changed kits when there was a direct clash and United generally changed to a white strip. Both clubs deviated from their usual kits on this day, with Sheffield United providing the most drastic of the changes. The team wore tangerine jerseys and socks with white shorts, while the Magpies changed their usual black-and-white stripes for a solid white shirt, although they kept their black shorts and white socks as normal.

On a warm March day, Newcastle kicked off, and Joe Shaw was called into early action to tackle White after he had beaten three men. The other Shaw, Graham, was then in action at the other end as Gerry Summers won a corner. United had a well-worked corner routine that involved Simpson cutting the ball back for Shaw to shoot from the edge of the area. This time, he met it on the volley but put it just wide.

Newcastle showed why their defence had been so porous, giving the ball away time and time again, and Bill Hodgson was able to pick up on one of the loose balls to play a 40-yard through-ball for Keith Kettleborough to find himself in space, only for Thomson to race across and put in a last-ditch challenge.

Minutes later, Summers, halfway into the Magpies' half on the left, put a superb deep cross towards the far side of the area.

Hodgson was there to meet it with his head, playing it back across. Newcastle keeper Mitchell came to claim it, but managed to drop it, and Russell was on hand to swivel his foot on to the ball and into the net. This meant that Russell had scored in every round of the cup run so far. Just eight minutes had been played, and the Blades had already breached the brittle Newcastle defence. Sheffield United's pressure since kick-off had been relentless, and this continued, with Newcastle seemingly unable to deal with it, or get any kind of attack of their own going.

Hughes on the right wing in particular was being given a tough time by Graham Shaw, being hit by hard tackle after hard tackle whenever he was on the ball, one of which landed him on the gravel track surrounding the pitch, earning Shaw a ticking off from the referee. Meanwhile, Joe Shaw was marking White out of the game, following him like a shadow.

Four minutes after the opener, a lightning attack put left-winger Ronnie Simpson in a position to shoot from the left of the area, which cannoned back off a defender straight back to him. Almost instinctively, he touched the rebound to the right, where Russell had found space, and blasted his, and United's, second goal past the keeper. In the 20th minute, Simpson again found himself in a good position down the left. Bringing the ball to the goal line, he had time and space to pick out a man, finding Hodgson at the far post with a chip-cross. Hodgson headed, but the ball hit the post. Out came the rebound, and in came Russell, who fired home to complete a 16-minute hat-trick.

Newcastle at last put an attack together, Ivor Allchurch (whose brother, Len, would join the Blades three weeks later) set up a chance for White. Alan Hodgkinson, United's England international keeper, rushed out to close him down, and this did the trick, White shooting wide of the post.

Either side of half-time, Russell had two good chances to score his fourth. In the first of them, Mitchell made a defensive slip, but Russell's eventual shot was blocked, then, in the first action of the second half, another defensive mix-up allowed Russell to get a shot away, but this time his shot was weak and easily saved.

Hughes finally got the better of Graham Shaw at the other end, cutting inside and blasting a goalbound shot, but Hodgkinson was somehow able to save it when a goal looked more likely. Newcastle were now getting more of the game, but the Blades were still the better side, particularly Keith Kettleborough, who was winning the ball from the front, finding space, and generally making a nuisance of himself for the Magpies' defence. This was creating space for Russell and Simpson to attack from midfield, and again this combination combined to create a chance for Russell, which he put wide. Simpson was then set up with a chance by 'Doc' Pace, but Bell managed to get in a last-ditch tackle before the Blades' winger could get the shot away.

The game entered the last ten minutes, and Newcastle finally breached the United defence. White picked up the ball on the left, and he put in a cross which found McGuigan, who had slipped his marker and headed home.

It was no more than a consolation, though.

United had, for the second time in this cup run, beaten First Division opposition away from home, and this time they had totally outclassed them.

Across Sheffield, Wednesday were having their best post-war season, eventually finishing as runners-up to champions Spurs, and also had a cup run of their own. While United were thrashing the Magpies, the Owls were held to a goalless draw at home to reigning league champions Burnley, so for the first time ever, both Sheffield teams went into the semi-final draw together. This time, unlike the next (and, to date, only other time, in 1993), the draw kept the two clubs apart, which, for one day after the Monday draw, created the prospect of an all-Sheffield final.

Home advantage for Burnley proved too much for Wednesday, though, and on the Tuesday, they lost 2-0 at Turf Moor. United, meanwhile, were to face Leicester, also flying high in the top division.

Russell's streak of scoring in every game was finally ended, as the two teams scrapped out a 0-0 at Elland Road, Leicester playing most of the game with ten men after an early injury and United having a last-minute goal disallowed controversially after Pace was adjudged to have handled the ball.

A replay at the City Ground brought the same goalless result, even with extra time and, after 90 minutes in a second replay at St. Andrew's, there had still been no goals in 300 minutes of football, although Hodgkinson had saved a penalty towards the end.

A goal finally came in the first half of extra time. Unfortunately, from a United perspective it fell to Leicester, and they added a second within five minutes to put the game beyond the Blades.

It had been a great cup run, with United showing themselves more than capable of handling themselves against First Division teams. There was little time for United to feel sorry for their cup exit as their first game after the semi-final defeat was against Liverpool, a point behind them in the promotion race.

What few suspected at the time, given that this was United's tenth trip to the semis, was that the demolition of Newcastle would be the Blades' last quarter-final win for 32 years. The result, and the tangerine kit, ensured that it would live in the memory for a long time. It would need to sustain memories of the FA Cup for some time for United supporters.

v Derby County 3-1

Football League Second Division
19 April 1961
Bramall Lane
Attendance: 21,773

SHEFFIELD UNITED	DERBY COUNTY
Hodgkinson	Oxford
Coldwell	Barrowcliffe
Shaw, G.	Conwell
Richardson	Parry
Shaw, J.	Moore
Summers	Upton
Allchurch	Powell
Russell	Hall
Pace	Curry
Hodgson	Hutchinson
Simpson	Hannigan
Manager: John Harris	Manager: Harry Storer

After four seasons of knocking on the door of promotion back to the First Division, but just being off the pace, things clicked in 1960/61. The team had led the table consistently from mid-September, but Ipswich had kept on their heels throughout.

The two teams met in March, three days after United had beaten First Division Newcastle away in the FA Cup quarter-finals. Ipswich ran out 3-1 winners at Bramall Lane, and the Suffolk club overtook the Blades at the top.

With nine games remaining, and Bill Shankly's Liverpool just three points behind them with two games in hand, manager John Harris knew there was no room for error. He turned to the transfer market, signing Welsh international left-winger Len Allchurch from Swansea. As new signings go, this was a belter! Allchurch scored on his debut against Leeds in a 2-1 win, which reignited the promotion push, and scored five goals in his first five games for the club.

Easter proved to be a key period. On the Saturday, five days after losing an FA Cup semi-final second replay to Leicester, a 1-1 draw with Liverpool at Bramall Lane left the Blades a point ahead of the Merseysiders. Three games followed in which Allchurch scored the winner, meanwhile Liverpool lost two of their next three, so United had moved five points clear with three games left. They now needed just two points to clinch promotion.

Their next opponents were Derby County, in the middle of their longest period outside of the top tier and sitting in mid-table. They had, however, beaten United 2-0 at the Baseball Ground earlier in the season.

United goalkeeper Alan Hodgkinson later wrote that, on the night at Bramall Lane, the team were 'pumped up, ready to win to secure the prize' while Derby lacked 'an edge to their game'. This was certainly evident in the opening stages of the game, keeper Ken Oxford being kept busy in the Derby goal.

Billy Russell broke through, only for his shot to be blocked by Conwell, and then Hodgson did the same, Conwell on hand again to block. It seemed only a matter of time, though, before United would open the scoring, and perhaps the only surprise was that it took 24 minutes to do so. Ronnie Simpson fed Brian Richardson the ball. In space, Richardson tried his luck from 30 yards, the shot was blocked, and the Rams' defence cleared, but only as far as Richardson. He played in Russell down the right. Russell's cross was a good one, and United's top scorer Derek Pace was on hand to volley home his 25th of the season.

The Blades kept the pressure up for the rest of the half, and came close to scoring again, but took just a single-goal lead into the break.

The eighth minute of the second half was an eventful one, particularly for Derby full-back Conwell. Firstly, he was reprimanded by the referee, then was hit by something thrown from the crowd, and finally, was in the wrong place at the wrong time when Len Allchurch put in a low cross from the right, and Conwell put the ball past his own keeper to double United's lead.

Although Hutchinson pulled one back for Derby to give them a glimmer of hope, United sealed the deal in the 71st minute. Again, Allchurch crossed from the right but this time it was met by a United man, 'Doc' Pace flinging himself at the ball to head past Oxford.

United were back at the top table after being bridesmaid for four years, and Hodgkinson attributed this to the manager above all else, stating that when he 'took over the reins from Joe Mercer he had assessed the team ... that Joe had left him and decided, "If it ain't broke, don't try and fix it." However, John had made subtle yet telling changes. For example, he signed Len Allchurch from Swansea.'

Allchurch had set up two of the goals against Derby, and he had certainly had a huge hand in United's promotion. The win also took them to the top of the division, but perhaps the team had celebrated a little too much, because three days later they lost 3-1 at Bristol Rovers while Ipswich overtook them and clinched their own promotion at the same time by beating Sunderland 4-0. In the end, United finished a point behind the Suffolk club, but in a season that saw United back in the First Division, and a run to the FA Cup semis, it mattered little to the club or its supporters.

v Sheffield Wednesday 2-0

Football League First Division
5 September 1964
Hillsborough
Attendance: 33,129

SHEFFIELD UNITED	SHEFFIELD WEDNESDAY
Hodgkinson	Springett
Badger	Hill
Shaw, G.	Megson
Richardson	McAnearney
Shaw, J.	Mobley
Matthewson	Young
Docherty	Finney
Kettleborough	Pearson
Jones	Quinn
Birchenall	Fantham
Hartle	Dobson
Manager: John Harris	Manager: Alan Brown

Since United's promotion back to the top flight in 1961, neither Sheffield team had finished outside of the top ten, which seems hard to believe from a 21st century vantage point. As United had challenged for promotion, in fact, Wednesday had challenged Spurs for the title, but manager Harry Catterick left in the March to take the Everton job, Wednesday took one win from their last four games, and Tottenham won the double, although Wednesday did have the consolation of qualifying for European competition for the first time.

Despite winning both games between the two Sheffield clubs in their first season back in the First Division, United failed to win the next four meetings, and Wednesday inflicted a heavy 3-0 defeat on them at Hillsborough in January 1964, which put them within four points of the top of the table.

Again, the Owls' season was to fall apart, this time in spectacular fashion. After manager Vic Buckingham resigned, three of their players were implicated in a match-fixing scandal which resulted in the club suspending them from football, and eventually they were banned from the game entirely.

John Harris's United, meanwhile, continued a policy of promoting from the youth team. The beginning of the 1964/65 season had been like a 'changing of the guard' from the old to the new. Ron Simpson, Derek Pace, and Len Allchurch, with almost 600 appearances between them, all lost their places to younger players in the first month and only Allchurch would appear again, and then only for two games later in the season.

Barry Hartle made the number 11 shirt his own after competing with Simpson for the past few seasons, and John Docherty had been brought back into the team after three seasons in the reserves. An even bigger surprise was the debut of blonde striker Alan Birchenall.

Birchenall, who had turned 19 on the opening day of the season, had scored 60 goals for the juniors in the Northern Intermediate League in the previous campaign, and was showing good form for the reserves in this one. Harris hoped that Birchenall would gel as a provider for another youth product, striker Mick Jones, who was just five months older but was already a first-team regular since the previous season.

Birchenall had not expected to play for the team, even when Harris invited him to travel with the team to Stoke for the midweek match before the derby. In the pre-match meal, thinking he had just been invited along to gain experience, he 'not only tucked into [his] own steaks but helped Joe Shaw and Cec Coldwell finish theirs!' before filling up on 'pounds of sweets and chocolates' on the team bus. At the ground, he was told he was playing and found his boots 'beneath the peg on which the no.10 shirt hung'.

Although he didn't score, United won 1-0, with Jones the scorer. The following Saturday, he was included again for the meeting with Wednesday.

As with many Sheffield derbies, the opening exchanges were even, with chances for both sides. United had, incidentally and unusually for the time, eschewed their traditional red-and-white stripes for an all-white strip. Their vocal support roared as Birchenall picked up an early through-ball from Kettleborough to find himself in a good position in the Kop-end penalty area, only for the linesman to raise his flag. Offside.

Birchenall was then involved at the back, clearing a ball into the area after Hodgkinson had pushed away Finney's cross.

United then had a chance. Another 19-year-old youth product, full-back Len Badger, put a free kick into the box which was met by the head of Mick Jones. The header, though, was saved under the bar by Springett. Springett had been the England first-choice keeper at the 1962 World Cup, ahead of Hodgkinson, but he found himself in trouble on the next Blades attack, missing a Hartle corner from the left but Don Megson was able to save him and clear the ball.

The clearest chance of the match so far now fell to Pearson, who latched on to a pinpoint pass from Quinn, steadied himself, and shot from 15 yards only to put the ball over the bar. After centre-half Reg Matthewson had put a speculative effort wide from 30 yards, Wednesday came back with another chance. Finney broke clear of Graham Shaw down the right and put in a great centre for Fantham to head the ball, but Hodgkinson was alert, well-positioned and able to make a clean catch. It was now Keith Kettleborough's turn to have a shot, which went wide, and then Fantham did the same at the other end, from just 12 yards. At this point in the game, the better chances were being created by Wednesday, and Hodgkinson had to make another good save, this time from Quinn, a low, hard shot which a diving Blades keeper turned around the post.

Teams need to take their chances, though, and Wednesday had created three already without finding the net. The football gods will punish teams that do not, and they did just that to the Owls now. Kettleborough put in a cross from the left, which was met by a Jones header. Springett was beaten, but the ball rebounded off the foot of the post. Birchenall, though, was alert, picked the ball up just inside the area and hit a low piledriver with his left. After 35 minutes United led, and the youngster, making just his second senior start, had got the goal.

He tried his luck again in the next attack, putting a first-time shot just wide, and then good defensive work by Kettleborough and Graham Shaw ensured that the Blades went into the break a goal ahead.

The second half started off in the same vein as the first, with attacks from both teams. Hartle forced a corner off Megson which came to nothing, then a high ball from Quinn beat Joe Shaw, only for Pearson to shoot straight at Hodgkinson.

Graham Shaw was having a great game at left-back, and tackled Finney as he was shaping to shoot from a Wednesday corner.

Still only ten minutes into the half, and another corner, this time to United. Hartle, from the left, took it, and there was Birchenall again to put it in the net, this time with his head, and double the Blades' lead, despite Hill's attempt to block it with his head.

The United supporters went crazy, and hailed their new hero, Alan Birchenall, the 'Sherman Tank'. While 'Sherman' had taken two chances, Wednesday had not taken any of theirs, and had missed another when Fantham teed up Quinn, whose shot scuffed the crossbar and went over. Frustration got the better of them, and Pearson tripped Joe Shaw when neither was close to the ball, leading to a booking.

Another chance came Wednesday's way, with 15 minutes left to play. Megson did well to meet a McAnearney ball with his head, and the shot looked goalbound, but Hodgkinson somehow managed to pull off a one-handed save to deny him.

Birchenall then had the chance for a hat-trick, only to be denied by a good save by Springett and Wednesday's day was summed up as Fantham latched on to a McAnearney free kick into the box, only to see his shot hit the underside of the bar and bounce clear.

A United win at Hillsborough always leaves a sweet taste in the mouth for Blades fans. This time, Birchenall was the hero. He would score seven in the next 11 league games, and four in the next three meetings with the Owls, a sure way to become a Blades legend.

After losing their first two games, United were now in sixth place and three games later would climb as high as second spot, before inconsistency hit. An eventual 19th-placed finish was a huge disappointment, especially when combined with Wednesday gaining revenge by winning 3-2 at Bramall Lane. Docherty would again lose his place in the first team, to be replaced by another young player, one going by the name of Alan Woodward.

Perhaps United's reliance on youth contributed to their inconsistency, but on a September afternoon in 1964, Blades fans were more than happy with the policy.

v Tottenham Hotspur 3-2

Football League First Division
26 February 1968
Bramall Lane
Attendance: 27,008

SHEFFIELD UNITED	TOTTENHAM HOTSPUR
Hodgkinson	Jennings
Badger	Kinnear
Shaw	Knowles
Munks	Mullery
Mallender	England
Wagstaff, B	Mackay
Woodward	Greaves
Carlin	Beal
Addison	Chivers
Currie	Venables
Reece	Jones
Manager: John Harris	Manager: Bill Nicholson

Once in a while, a player makes a debut that has the fans buzzing about their new prospect and the only topic of conversation in the pubs after, and at work and school the next day, are about their new 'star' player.

Some turn out to be flashes in the pan. Centre-forward John Turley, for instance, scored on his Blades debut in 1957, also scored in the next two games, but quickly lost his touch, was dropped and only played a total of five games for the club. Vas Borbokis tore Sunderland apart on his debut in 1997 and became a crowd favourite, but had moved on within two years.

Possibly the greatest Blades debut, both in terms of performance on the night, but also the long-term impact of the player, was that of a young Anthony William Currie, on a Monday night in February 1968.

United were in their seventh consecutive season in the top flight and had never been in any real danger of relegation for the previous six. The club had, however, spent money on a new two-tier stand at the Bramall Lane end in 1966, so a book-balancing decision was made to cash in on top scorer Mick Jones, selling him to Leeds for £100,000 in September 1967. The M1 motorway was being extended from the Midlands to Leeds, and it seemed that

United took this as cue to start sending all of their best players up it, as we will see.

Two months after Jones's departure, Alan Birchenall was sold to Chelsea for the same fee, at his own request as he felt he was worth more than United were paying him. The club, having sold their two main strikers, were now inevitably drawn into a relegation scrap, although manager John Harris, now in his ninth full season at the helm, genuinely felt that the players were good enough to stay in the division.

Based on this, he continued to recruit for the future, and he saw potential in an 18-year-old player at Third Division Watford. The two clubs agreed a fee of £26,500 for the player, Tony Currie, on the basis that the transfer go through after Watford had exited the FA Cup. After the Hornets beat non-league Hereford in the second round, fate drew them against the Blades in the third. United won 1-0, Watford were true to their word and the transfer went through on 1 February.

Harris saw Currie as one for the future, and put him in the reserves initially, but a cup run, which saw them make the quarter-finals, put pressure on a small squad. Harris pressed a cup-tied Currie into service for the league game at home to Spurs.

Tottenham were one of the teams of the 1960s, having won the double in 1961, the FA Cup in 1967, and finishing every season of the decade in the top ten places. Of the starting XI in the Bramall Lane game, nine of the team had won international caps, and one more (Chivers) would go on to win his in the future. They also boasted arguably the greatest English goalscorer of his or, some might say, any generation in Jimmy Greaves.

The 14 places that separated the two teams wasn't evident as the game began, though, as United spent the first 20 minutes on the front foot. This was in spite of an early knock to winger Alan Woodward which meant he had to play the rest of the game with a strapped-up ankle.

Despite United's early dominance, there were no goals after 20 minutes, but then their left-back Bernard Shaw was robbed of possession by Chivers, who teed the ball up for Greaves to shoot. Alan Hodgkinson, the United keeper, by now in his 15th season with the club, managed to get a hand to Greaves's first-time shot and turn it around the post for a corner.

The corner came in, and Greaves again shot. This time the shot was closed down, but the United defence failed to clear. For a third time in a row, the ball fell to Greaves, this time closer to goal, and this time he made no mistake to make it 1-0 to Spurs.

Greaves's goal aside, United had dominated the game and dictated the play. Currie was at the crux of it all, combining great intelligence, both in possession and off the ball, with youthful energy. This was enabling those around him to play better than they had done recently, too, notably Gil Reece and Colin Addison.

Nine minutes after the Greaves goal, Addison followed up a nice run with an inch-perfect through-ball to Barry Wagstaff. Wagstaff's shot was blocked, but the rebound fell straight back to him, and he was able to finish on the second attempt. The scores were level, and Spurs' lead had lasted for just nine minutes.

United continued to attack, forcing Mackay and Knowles in particular to make mistakes, and chances continued to come. Spurs' 22-year-old Northern Irish keeper, Pat Jennings, was tested by Addison and Currie, while shots from Wagstaff and Reece narrowly missed the target.

In the 44th minute, United countered a rare Spurs attack. Chivers lost possession in the area, and the defence cleared the ball to midfielder David Munks. He crossed from the right, his centre met beautifully by the head of Currie. The header was accurate, powerful, and flew into the net. It was no more than the Blades debutant had deserved, and it meant that United led at half-time, 2-1.

United continued to boss the game in the second half, and almost doubled their lead when Addison spurned a good opportunity to score, putting a clear-cut chance wide of the upright, but they finally got the third goal their play deserved after 73 minutes. A poor clearance by Cliff Jones fell straight to Reece on the left wing. Shooting from an angle, his shot curled into the far top corner of Jennings's goal.

Unitedites know that their team never like them to be comfortable though, and Chivers pulled a goal back seven minutes later.

Hearts were in mouths minutes later when Greaves had a good chance, but Hodgkinson pulled off a good save to deny

Tottenham any points. A draw would have been a travesty, though, as Spurs hadn't deserved anything from the game. United had been magnificent, and the man pulling the strings all night was Tony Currie.

His name was on the lips of the Blades supporters, and the headlines of the local papers, and this was certainly not a flash-in-the-pan debut. He would spend eight years at the club, and be selected for England honours during that time. In United's 125th anniversary year, he won a poll amongst supporters asking who the club's greatest-ever player was, and the South Stand (ironically, the stand that would indirectly result in his sale to Leeds) was renamed in his honour.

Unfortunately, he couldn't save the club from relegation in 1967/68, despite the heroics against Spurs. Not for the last time in Blades' history, a final day defeat to Chelsea sent them down, and the team would be rebuilt over the next few years into one that is probably the most affectionately remembered United team of them all. At its heart, one Tony Currie.

v Cardiff City 5-1

Football League Second Division
27 April 1971
Bramall Lane
Attendance: 42,963

SHEFFIELD UNITED	CARDIFF CITY
Hope	Eadie
Badger	Carver
Hemsley	Bell
Flynn	Sutton
Colquhoun	Murray
Hockey	Derrett
Woodward	Gibson
Salmons	Clark
Dearden	Phillips (Woodruff)
Currie	Warboys
Reece	King
Manager: John Harris	Manager: Jimmy Scoular

After relegation in 1968, any hopes of an immediate return to the top flight soon disappeared, as, under new manager Arthur Rowley, United limped to a disappointing ninth place. Rowley was moved on. An exciting, attacking team was coming together, featuring star midfielder Tony Currie and now back under manager John Harris, and the team challenged for promotion in the 1969/70 season, until a run of four straight defeats in March killed off any hopes.

The 1970/71 season began slowly, despite a win in the League Cup over First Division leaders Leeds, but they stayed in touch with the chasing pack. The board backed the manager, signing goalkeeper John Hope from Newcastle and tough midfielder Trevor Hockey from Birmingham, whose job was simply to 'win the ball and give it to Currie'. This he did, and more, becoming a Bramall Lane legend in a just two-year spell at the club.

The team moved to the top of the table in February, but just five points separated them and eighth-placed Norwich, the race for promotion was so tight. Two successive defeats against fellow promotion chasers, Carlisle then Hull, and then three successive 0-0 draws in April (the last at Hillsborough) left many fans fearing a repeat of the previous season, but then came two successive wins which put United back into second place.

One point behind them, with a game in hand, were Cardiff City, who travelled to Sheffield for a Tuesday evening game. A win for United would put them three points clear and in pole position to secure second place, a draw or a defeat would mean they were dependent on the Welshmen dropping points in their last two games. In a nutshell, it was a must-win for the Blades.

Cardiff had made a piece of history earlier in the season by reaching the last eight of the European Cup-Winners' Cup, beating Real Madrid 1-0 at Ninian Park, qualifying as they did in those days through winning the Welsh Cup.

They had challenged for promotion throughout the season, despite the sale of goalscorer John Toshack to Liverpool. He had been replaced by former Wednesday striker Alan Warboys, who would also later have a spell with the Blades.

The largest crowd in four years crammed into Bramall Lane to watch this crunch match. United, kicking towards the Kop, started well, and should have taken the lead in the first three minutes. A through-ball from Hockey beat the offside trap and found Gil Reece, who should have scored, but put the ball wide.

Three minutes later an Alan Woodward corner was cleared and, as the players ran back towards the middle, Hockey cleverly played the ball forward. Again, he beat the Cardiff trap and, this time, his pass found Bill Dearden. As the goalkeeper was caught in two minds about whether to come out to meet him, Dearden shot past him and into the Cardiff goal to put United ahead.

Following the Blades' onslaught of the opening minutes, Cardiff started to exert themselves on the game, their creative midfielder Ian Gibson spraying accurate passes in the manner which the Blades' support was used to seeing from Tony Currie.

After Warboys was booked for a robust challenge on United keeper John Hope, resulting in him requiring emergency stitches in his nose, Derrett then latched on to a Gibson through-ball and unleashed a shot. Thankfully for United, it flew over the bar.

In the 33rd minute, United were awarded a free kick on the left. Currie's ball into the box was a beauty, finding Len Badger, whose flick-on went to John Flynn. The centre-half twisted his body and headed into the goal; 2-0. The goal had really come against the run of play, and Cardiff continued to boss the midfield. Phillips had an effort cleared off the line, but eventually their play got the goal it deserved. Hemsley, defensive hero moments earlier, now turned villain, as his mistake presented an opening for Derrett on the edge of the United area. His shot would probably have been saved by Hope, had it not taken a wicked deflection off Hockey and into the goal, with moments left before the end of the half.

At half-time, United led by a goal, the game still on a knife-edge. Cardiff had, perhaps, been the better team in the first half, and an equaliser would put their destiny firmly in their own hands. Captain Eddie Colquhoun, acknowledging after the game that, despite United's lead, Cardiff had been stronger in the first half than the Blades, said that, at half-time 'we decided to go out and start a new match.'

They did just that, and, within ten minutes of the restart, doubled their lead. Woodward, always dangerous from corners, swung one in from the left. Currie, standing virtually on the line, glanced it into the net with his head. The Cardiff players complained that the keeper had been impeded, but the goal stood.

Just 11 minutes later, Murray, Cardiff's uncompromising centre-back, misplaced a pass which Woodward pounced on, heading the ball on to Reece. Reece, Cardiff-born and jettisoned by the Bluebirds when he was 20, latched on to Woodward's header and shot with power from the edge of the area and into the top left-hand corner of the goal, despite Eadie getting his fingertips to the ball.

The score was 4-1 and the game, and with it the promotion challenge, was beyond Cardiff now. Their heads dropped while United still attacked, and with some style, a 40-yard pass from Currie picking out a wonderful run from Dearden.

Beating the last man, Murray, Dearden shot past the oncoming keeper, only for his shot to clip the top of the crossbar and go over. He got another chance soon after, though, with nine minutes of the game remaining, this time being picked out by Reece in space on the left. Dearden cut inside and put a low shot across the goal, and into the far corner of the net. After the match, Dearden said that he felt 'thrilled' with his two goals, although he was slightly regretful that the crossbar had denied him a hat-trick.

The final whistle came, and young supporters streamed on to the pitch to assemble in front of the John Street stand and cheer their heroes. Dearden, though, warned the team not to 'get carried away. There's Saturday's match still to come yet.' Promotion was not secured, United now needed just a point at home to Watford to secure second place, or for Cardiff not to win one of their last two games. He need not have worried, though. In the Watford game, United led 2-0 at half-time, and added a third in the second half. Cardiff's result was now irrelevant and United were promoted back to the top flight.

Although promotion was clinched in the Watford game, it was the demolition of their closest promotion rivals, in front of the biggest crowd of the season, that would live longest in the memories of supporters of the era.

v Leeds United 3-0

26 Football League First Division
17 August 1971
Bramall Lane
Attendance: 40,725

SHEFFIELD UNITED	LEEDS UNITED
Hope	Sprake
Badger	Reaney
Hemsley	Madeley
Flynn	Bremner
Colquhoun	Charlton
Hockey	Hunter
Woodward	Lorimer
Salmons	Clarke
Dearden	Belfitt
Currie	Giles
Scullion	Bates
Manager: John Harris	Manager: Don Revie

One month earlier, as the Blades team prepared themselves for life back in the top flight, the decision had been made that Bramall Lane would become a four-sided stadium, and cricket would no longer be played at the old ground.

The United board felt that this was necessary if United were to become a permanent fixture in the First Division, as gate receipts were half of those for similar crowds at other clubs due to the restrictions that an 'open' side of the ground put on ticket pricing. The money simply wasn't there unless a stand was built on that side. This was reflected in the fact that John Harris made no new signings in the summer and was using the team that got the club promoted to keep them there.

It certainly wasn't short of attacking talent, though. The obvious stars were Tony Currie and Alan Woodward, ably supported by the likes of Bill Dearden, Geoff Salmons and Trevor Hockey. A lack of investment did mean a lack of strength in depth, but, with his first-choice XI, Harris had a team that could take the game to any team in the league, and they got off to a flyer. By half-time in the opening game at home to Southampton, they led 2-0, eventually winning 3-1. United's next three games, though, were against the 1969, 1970, and 1971 champions respectively, namely Leeds, Everton and Arsenal, the first game coming just three days after the Southampton game. A Yorkshire derby against one of the top teams of the era drew in almost 15,000 more spectators than the meeting with the Saints.

This really was Leeds's heyday as a club. Until manager Don Revie had taken over in 1961, they had yo-yoed between the top two divisions, never finishing higher than fifth in the top flight and winning one Second Division title in 1924. Revie took over and turned them into a force in English football, although they would often be criticised for negative, dirty tactics, earning the epitaph 'Dirty Leeds' that survives to this day. After getting into the top flight in 1964, they had finished in the top four every season, winning the league in 1969 and the Fairs Cup (now the Europa League) in 1971, with household names such as Jack Charlton, Billy Bremner, Norman Hunter, Johnny Giles and Peter Lorimer.

As the Blades had chased promotion in the spring of 1971, Leeds had pushed Arsenal all the way for the title, and they had felt aggrieved at an offside decision not being given, resulting in a goal being scored against them against West Brom which cost them the game. They were correct to feel hard done by, although the goal would have not even been in question under modern conditions of 'not interfering with play'. Arsenal won the league by a point.

Leeds travelled to Bramall Lane on a Tuesday night in August, then, as a force to be reckoned with. Their scout, Maurice Lindley, had been at the Southampton game, though, and described the Blades as 'the best team to leave the Second Division in years'. Sheffield United could also take some confidence from a surprise win over Leeds in the League Cup a year earlier.

The first half was fairly uneventful, with Leeds perhaps showing their top-flight nous and starting to become dominant, particularly in midfield, as the half drew to a close.

Unitedites may have been worried that Leeds would continue to exert their authority in the second half, but these fears were soon allayed as the Blades took the lead in the 55th minute. Kicking towards the Bramall Lane end, Bill Dearden made a trademark surge forward and won a corner on the left. Woodward kicked in one of his inswinging corners which keeper Sprake missed. John Flynn, up from defence for the set-piece, leapt above Jack Charlton at the far post and headed the ball into the middle of the goal.

Seven minutes later, Leeds felt they should have been awarded a penalty. Ted Hemsley's mistake let in Lorimer on the right and with only keeper Hope to beat. Lorimer rounded him, but then was sent crashing to the ground. It looked like a penalty to everyone, except, most importantly, the referee.

As the game wore on, United became more defensive, the defenders and midfielders struggling to find forwards to pass to. Leeds came at United, two shots going narrowly wide. Then, in the last ten minutes, came a second penalty appeal. Charlton's shot was charged down, Leeds claimed handball, but again, the referee awarded nothing. This led to Leeds players surrounding and pushing the referee in the face. Remarkably, no bookings resulted from this.

Perhaps feeling hard done by, and perhaps losing concentration, Leeds were then hit by a sucker-punch, as a now-rare United attack resulted in the second goal. The waspish Stewart Scullion made a run down the left and sent in a low cross, which both Sprake and Reaney misjudged. Dearden, though, did not, and arrived at the back post to put it home. With four minutes to go, the Blades led 2-0.

Woodward's corners had caused Sprake problems all night. He had missed four of six including the opening goal. Two minutes after United's second goal, he missed another, Flynn again winning it at the far post but this time heading it back across goal where Eddie Colquhoun, surrounded by Leeds shirts, got his head to it and into the net, as he himself was spun around in the scrimmage.

The game was over as a contest now, with 88 minutes on the clock, but this did not stop Lorimer from putting in a high tackle on Currie which resulted in a brawl. Again, no bookings were forthcoming.

Currie had been imperious for the second half, overshadowing his more famous midfield opponents, and the Lorimer tackle personified the perception of the two teams, certainly amongst the Blades faithful. This was a victory for the Sheffield United entertainers over the cynical 'Dirty Leeds'.

Leeds would recover from this defeat, and would go on to win the FA Cup at the end of the season. Two days after the final, they played Wolves needing just a point to win the league. They lost 2-1, handing Brian Clough's Derby the title.

After the victory over Leeds, United would go on to to win six and draw two of the next eight, putting them three points clear at the top at the end of September. After losing to a piece of George Best magic at Old Trafford, the lack of squad depth started to show, and United finished in a (still respectable) tenth place. For a spell at the beginning of the season, though, they were the kings of the land and the 'entertainers' had repelled 'Dirty Leeds'.

v Arsenal 5-0

27

Football League First Division
4 September 1973
Bramall Lane
Attendance: 27,839

SHEFFIELD UNITED	ARSENAL
McAlister	Wilson
Badger	Batson
Hemsley	Rice
Flynn	Blockley
Colquhoun	Storey
Eddy	McNab
Woodward	Armstrong
Salmons	Ball
Dearden	Kelly
Currie	Kennedy
Bone	George
Manager: John Harris	Manager: Bertie Mee

Sometimes, it's almost as if the football gods have written the script.

In United's first season back in the top, 1971/72, Arsenal had travelled to Sheffield at the end of January, with United in fifth place and a point ahead of the Gunners in the table, having lost just one game at Bramall Lane.

It was the fourth time the teams had met in the season. United had won 1-0 at Highbury in the league and then forced a replay in the League Cup, which they won 2-0.

Few, then, expected the result that followed in the league meeting at Bramall Lane. In fact, United had dominated the opening 15 minutes of the game, Bob Wilson pulling off a couple of fine saves, but then a nightmare afternoon began for the Blades' defence, and keeper John Hope in particular, as Arsenal put five past them. Charlie George scored a hat-trick, but it was Arsenal's World Cup-winning England midfielder, Alan Ball, who is most remembered, capping off a fine midfield performance, and adding insult to injury, by sitting on the ball in the centre-circle while the ball was still in play, in an ultimate piece of showboating.

The 5-0 defeat had been United's biggest home loss for 21 years. United won just four more games in the season and dropped to tenth while Arsenal finished fifth.

Hope was replaced in goal for the 1972/73 season by youth product Tom McAlister, and United again finished mid-table, while Arsenal had challenged Liverpool for the title, finishing runners-up. The two teams met again early the next season, with no new additions to the Blades line-up. Both teams had won just one of their first three games, but Arsenal had scored five goals to United's two. What was to follow would become the stuff of Sheffield United legend.

Anyone arriving late to the stadium that evening would have missed the onslaught, as United blew Arsenal away in a scintillating first 17 minutes.

The first goal took just 35 seconds. Arsenal kicked off, Tony Currie won the ball from Charlie George, and Keith Eddy got the ball out wide to Alan Woodward, racing down the right. Woodward's cross was fast, accurate and met by the oncoming Bill Dearden to put United ahead.

Eight minutes later after Dearden's opener, Currie won a free kick on the edge of the area. Taking it himself, he teed up Woodward to shoot from 22 yards. Wilson saw it too late, and the Blades were two goals to the good. Arsenal, Storey especially, just couldn't handle Currie, and even fouling him didn't work. In the tenth minute, Currie got in on the scoring act himself, playing a quick one-two with Dearden in midfield and then shooting from 25 yards, the ball flying in between Wilson and his left post.

After just ten minutes of play, all of the United forwards and wingers had scored except for Jim Bone, who had joined United from Norwich the previous season. Now he completed the set, cutting inside and unleashing a cracker past Wilson. Only 17 minutes, and United were 4-0 up. It could have been five soon after, Dearden hitting the post with a shot.

With the Blades so far ahead, sweet revenge was now served, as Tony Currie repeated Ball's trick and sat on the ball.

'We were leading 4-0,' Currie later described 'so it was just my chance to get my own back. The thing is he did it on the halfway line and I did it in our box. When I got up, I tripped over the ball and they almost scored from it!'

One of the ballboys that day was future United player and caretaker manager Steve Thompson, who later recalled that not only did Currie sit on the ball, but also 'beckoned Alan Ball towards him. Alan ran at him and TC nutmegged him.'

Arsenal, to their credit, didn't give up completely, Ball hitting the post and Ted Hemsley having to clear an effort off the line, but United still dominated and created chances of their own. Wilson pulled off a save from a decent Woodward effort, and then, in the 61st minute, Geoff Salmons played Currie in to shoot home with power from the edge of the area for United's fifth.

Armstrong hit the post for Arsenal in the last minute, but they could easily have conceded two or three more, and an 8-2 scoreline would not have been a bad reflection on the action. A week later, the Gunners won the return fixture 1-0. Both teams would finish mid-table.

It would be the highlight of the season for Blades fans. Currie had further cause to celebrate later in the month when scoring his first England goal against Austria. I was born in 1973, so never got to see Tony Currie play, apart from in a testimonial game in the mid-1980s.

In a pub conversation with a decades-long Wednesday fan when I was old enough to buy him a pint, I asked him who was the greatest player he ever saw in the flesh. With no hesitation, he said 'Tony Currie.' High praise indeed from an Owl!

Say Currie's name to any Blades fan of that era and they will go misty-eyed and tell you of the flowing locks, 50-yard passes to the feet of his team-mates, blowing kisses to the crowd, 'You Can Do Magic' playing on the tannoy, and also of the day he sat on the ball against Arsenal.

v West Ham United 3-2

28

Football League First Division
22 March 1975
Bramall Lane
Attendance: 25,527

SHEFFIELD UNITED	WEST HAM UNITED
Brown	Day
Badger	Coleman
Bradford	Lampard
Eddy	McDowell
Colquhoun	Taylor, T.
Flynn	Lock
Woodward	Jennings
Speight	Paddon
Cammack	Taylor, A.
Currie	Brooking
Field	Gould
Manager: Ken Furphy	Manager: John Lyall

There are no doubt numerous cracking games throughout United's long history that have not stayed in the collective memory because they were not promotion clinchers, or big cup games, and the memories have died out as the people who were there on the day have dwindled in number.

For the vast majority of games before the late 1980s, there were no TV or video cameras present. Indeed United did not feature on a live free-to-air match until 1993. Highlight appearances were limited to a handful of games each season. Not being a Manchester United or a Liverpool counted against them, as did the fact that they weren't based close to the broadcasters' headquarters in London.

When United faced the Hammers in March 1975, it had been just over a year since a United home game had been included in the *Match of the Day* line-up, but the BBC's timing was immaculate. Because it was captured by their cameras, but also because of one magical piece of play by a Blades icon and a legendary spot of TV commentary by John Motson, this is a game that is not only fondly remembered, it is an essential part of the Sheffield United story.

At the start of the 1974/75 season, manager John Harris had been moved 'upstairs' after 13 years in charge, and had been replaced by Ken Furphy, who had been Tony Currie's first manager at Watford. The new South Stand was due to open at the beginning of the next season, and the cost of its building meant that there was little to spend on the squad. Many fans, then, expected a tough season, but the team played above themselves, in one of the most open First Divisions in memory. Between the beginning of October and mid-November the Blades went from 5th to 13th and back up to 5th again. By the time the BBC cameras rolled into Bramall Lane, they were ninth, but just two points from third spot and five points off the top.

West Ham were just two points behind them in 11th. Ron Greenwood had continued the tradition of the Hammers 'academy', with the likes of Trevor Brooking, Frank Lampard senior and keeper Mervyn Day coming up through the ranks, but Greenwood had taken the England job in pre-season. Another West Ham youth product, youth-team manager, John Lyall, was appointed to replace him. After a slow start, the goals began flying in, including 14 in three games in September, and the Hammers had also progressed to the FA Cup semi-finals.

Two good, attacking teams met at Bramall Lane in front of the cameras.

United were missing Bill Dearden and Ted Hemsley through injury, but West Ham were missing their captain, Billy Bonds.

Kicking with a strong wind behind them towards the Shoreham Street end of the ground, the Hammers created the first chance in the opening minute, a long kick from Day being misjudged by Woodward, leaving Gould free on the left, but a diagonal shot was easily dealt with by Jim Brown in the United goal. They attacked again, Alan Taylor with a lovely turn to beat Eddy and unleashing a hard shot which caused Brown to make a fine save, palming it around the post.

West Ham had dominated the opening exchanges, and they got their reward after just eight minutes. From a poor clearance, McDowell hit a first-time pass to Alan Taylor on the right. Taylor did well to keep it in play, sliding the ball down the flank where McDowell had run into the area. Playing a square ball across the box, Gould met it and slotted home.

From the kick-off, United won a throw on the left deep into the West Ham half. Tony Currie switched play to the right, picking out Alan Woodward with a weighted cross-field pass over the edge of the area. Woodward controlled the ball, stopping it dead before taking the ball past Paddon and firing it towards the near post. Steve Cammack went for the ball, with a West Ham defender and keeper Day both attempting to clear, but the United player managed to screw it across goal where a waiting Currie was able to poke it in from a yard out.

West Ham's lead had lasted for just one minute. Currie and Cammack combined again. Currie's superb backheel this time set up Cammack who struck it perfectly, only for Day to pull off a fine diving save.

Currie was at his imperious best, spraying passes around and keeping the West Ham defenders busy, and a crucial challenge from Gould robbed Colquhoun of a good chance that the Blades maestro had set up.

Despite Currie's magic, West Ham regained the lead in the 29th minute, or, rather, the lead was handed to them. A header into the box from Paddon was met by a skewed overhead kick from Jennings, the ball looping high into the air. Brown came to claim what looked like an easy catch, as players moved back into position expecting a kick-out, but Brown took his eye off the ball and fumbled it into the net.

Currie again endeavoured to get United back into the match. After he was fouled by McDowell, he took the free kick himself, setting up John Flynn, who should have scored, then the rebound fell to Cammack, who also managed to miss. West Ham took their lead into the break, but the scores were almost level after a minute of the restart. Woodward crossed, and Tony Field launched himself at the ball, missing it by a fraction.

It was all United now, and they got a deserved equaliser in the 58th minute. An accurate long throw by Brown found Cammack in space in the middle of the park. From 40 yards out, he hit a diagonal pass that found Woodward on the left at the edge of the area. Woodward had two defenders ahead of him, with Eddy in space at the far post and Cammack continuing his run into the area, but Woodward chose to go it alone, beating both defenders and hitting a low shot just inside the near post.

Just 12 minutes later, United almost took the lead. Eddy's long clearance found Woodward, whose shot was pushed into the path of Cammack. He hit it well, but the shot cannoned back off the bar.

Although the Blades were level, they had spurned some good chances, and were almost punished for this when Alan Taylor latched on to a poor back-pass from Mick Speight, but Brown threw himself at the legs of the oncoming defender to claim the ball.

Another chance came United's way, Currie beating two defenders before unleashing a powerful shot. Again, the bar came to the Hammers' rescue.

The scene was set, and the time had come, for one of the most iconic moments in Blades history, with 11 minutes remaining. It began with Currie in defence, blocking a Gould pass which would have rolled out of play, had Woodward not chased it down, tapping it back towards Currie.

Just inside the West Ham half, on the right, Currie looked up and, seeing three West Ham defenders between him and the goal, drove forwards with the ball.

As the first defender challenged him, Currie dropped his left shoulder, dragging the ball towards the centre as the defender gave chase. With the ball at his feet at the edge of the area, he swerved this way and that, like a boxer waiting for his chance to punch. Another feint and he saw his opening, placing a low, rolling, but accurate shot just inside the bottom left-hand post.

'What about that?' cried John Motson on the *Match of the Day* commentary later that evening, 'A quality goal by a quality player ... his second of the match, and they don't come any better,' as colour TV sets around the country beamed Currie's blonde locks flowing across his red-and-white striped shoulders as he ran to blow kisses to the United faithful.

In the last ten minutes of the game, Day was called on to produce two fine saves, first from Cammack and lastly, fittingly, from Currie.

The scoreline possibly flattered West Ham, but it mattered little.

The names of the two scorers on the day – Currie and Woodward – are forever linked in Blades' hearts, and this would be the last time their names would appear together on the scoresheet. United put in more good performances before the end of the season, beating Stoke at home then Everton away on consecutive Saturdays to end each of their title hopes. With a game in hand on the rest of the league, a win away at Birmingham would have seen them qualify for European competition for the first time. They drew 0-0, missed out and were deservedly relegated the following season. After eight years of wonderful memories, Currie moved on to Leeds.

Everything had come together in that 79th minute against West Ham to produce what is, for a number of Blades, THE most memorable moment.

Tony Field had, arguably, scored a better goal against Ipswich earlier in the season, captured by Yorkshire Television, but this was Anthony William Currie, on *Match of the Day*, with Motson's memorable voice and words, capping off another great performance in red-and-white stripes by the maestro.

v Liverpool 1-0

League Cup Second Round
28 August 1978
Bramall Lane
Attendance: 35,753

SHEFFIELD UNITED	LIVERPOOL
Conroy	Clemence
Cutbush	Neal
Garner	Thompson
Keeley	Hughes
Matthews	Kennedy, A.
Speight	Case (Fairclough,70)
Woodward	McDermott
Stainrod	Souness
Finnieston (Franks,64)	Kennedy, R.
Hamson	Heighway
Sabella	Dalglish
Manager: Harry Haslam	Manager: Bob Paisley

In July 1971, the decision was made to end cricket at Bramall Lane and build a new stand on the Cherry Street side of the ground, to improve revenues and allow United to compete with the top teams. First, though, the club needed to cover the cost of the stand, and this required First Division crowds.

Relegation in 1976, then, was a disaster for the club, and the inevitable sale of Tony Currie to Leeds to reduce the debt broke supporters' hearts. Attendances dropped, and two mid-table finishes in the Second Division followed, the second being a 12th-place finish which was at that point the club's lowest-ever finish in the Football League.

United fans were slightly heartened at the beginning of the 1978/79 season by the club spending a record fee of £160,000 on an Argentinian player called Alex Sabella, having been rebuffed in their attempts to buy an unknown teenager called Diego Maradona.

Sabella was an exciting, skillful player, and scored the equaliser in United's third game of the season, by which point the team had won one, drawn one and lost one. This was hardly an opening to get the pulses racing.

Something that did get the fans buzzing, though, was the draw for the second round of the League Cup. The first round had taken place before the league programme had kicked off, so United were already aware that they would be hosting Liverpool before their season began.

Younger readers may not understand just how huge this was. In the previous six seasons Liverpool had been league champions three times, runners-up in the other three years, and were reigning European Champions, having won the trophy in consecutive seasons. They showed no signs of relenting their pursuit of silverware as the new season kicked off, winning their first three games, scoring nine in the process.

Unlike with today's cup games, teams then put out their best teams as often as they could. The Liverpool line-up against the Blades was unchanged from a 4-1 win at Maine Road two days earlier.

This, then, was the best team of the 1970s, and one of the best to ever grace English football. Indeed, there are cases to be made for at least two of them (Dalglish and Souness) to be considered the best ever in their respective positions in the English game. Even their substitute, David Fairclough, was a specialist in the sub's role.

They rolled into town on a Monday night in August, fully expected to deliver a cricket score against a decidedly average second-tier outfit.

Starting for the Blades was Gary Hamson, who had made his debut for United two years earlier, at the time the club's youngest-ever debutant at 16 years and five months. He had celebrated his 19th birthday just four days before the Liverpool game, but admitted 'we expected to get thrashed. Liverpool were a brilliant team, full of great players.'

As expected, they dominated from kick-off, perhaps displaying a level of complacency that meant they never really got out of second gear.

The first half turned out to be a bit of a damp squib. The only real talking point was when United were awarded a free kick, and the Liverpool wall failed to retreat the required ten yards. As a result, the referee booked four players at the same time – Case, McDermott, Neal and Dalglish.

United survived to half-time, but only because Liverpool hadn't got going yet. Blades manager Harry Haslam had, according to

Hamson, set out to shackle Liverpool with every player being man-marked tightly. 'I was given the task of man-marking Terry McDermott. I followed him all over the place ... [and] must have done a decent job because halfway through the second half he turned and said "Just **** off!"'

Their manager Paisley must have given them a rocket at half-time, though, because they came out of the traps like a team possessed. Within ten minutes of the restart, they created eight clear-cut chances to score, but a mixture of bad luck and a combination of three United players – keeper Steve Conroy and defenders John Matthews and John Cutbush, somehow meant the score was still 0-0 after these relentless ten minutes.

Conroy was a Blades youth product who had been reserve keeper behind Jim Brown, but now found himself thrust into first choice after Brown was tempted to the US to join Detroit Express. Matthews, a centre-half, had been signed in the summer from Arsenal for a not-insignificant sum of £90,000, while right-back Cutbush had come from Fulham the year before.

The first of the eight Liverpool chances in those ten minutes fell to Heighway, but Matthews was there to clear off the line with keeper Conroy beaten.

Next, Conroy pulled off a brilliant save from a Ray Kennedy shot, then did it again from a headed effort from the same player.

Case was the next to get his chance, but his cracking shot from distance went inches wide.

Following this, Dalglish collected the ball with his back to goal, turned, and shot, only for his effort to narrowly clear the crossbar.

Conroy pulled off a third good save in a matter of minutes, this time from McDermott, then John Cutbush cleared a Souness effort off the line.

The last of the succession of chances fell again to Ray Kennedy, who put just wide. It had been a remarkable passage of play, but somehow a goal had evaded the European champions.

The pressure continued, although not quite at the same level of intensity as those first ten minutes of the second half, but United still were not getting a look-in. Conroy, though, kept them in it. A fine save from Alan Kennedy was followed pretty much immediately with another from Liverpool's other Kennedy, Ray.

All of the second-half play had been in the United half at the Bramall Lane end but, with ten minutes to go, the Blades finally mustered an attack, resulting in a goalmouth scramble. The ball was half-cleared to Gary Hamson, who recalls '[Sabella] squeezed the ball to me on the edge of the 18-yard area, I had one touch and belted it,' his left-foot shot flying past the outstretched leg of Phil Thompson and then beating Clemence into the net.

Hamson had celebrated his 19th birthday just four days before the Liverpool game, and now the Unitedites behind the goal had something to celebrate with him.

To say the scoreline flattered United would be a huge understatement – had it not been for a combination of Conroy, Matthews and Cutbush, it could have been a hammering. Regardless, United saw out the last ten minutes. They had, somehow, beaten the team of the decade.

The following Saturday, Liverpool beat Spurs 7-0 at Anfield (the highlights of which are well worth watching online, especially the seventh goal) and went on to win the title, the European Super Cup and also reach the semi-finals of the FA Cup, although they failed in their quest to win three European Cups in a row after eventual champions Forest knocked them out.

The Blades, meanwhile, lost their next game 2-0, at home to Terry Venables's Palace, and they ended the season with relegation to the third tier for the first time in the club's history. Hamson was sold to Leeds in the summer, to join Jones and Currie on the ever-growing list of players sold by United to the Elland Road club.

With United top of the table in Division Three in December 1979, Conroy suffered a broken arm. United's form imploded after this, and they dropped out of the promotion race, including suffering probably the most humiliating defeat in their history on the Boxing Day. The memory of toppling the mighty Reds would need to sustain Blades fans for a few seasons to come, when highlights were hard to come by.

v Darlington 2-0

Football League Fourth Division
15 May 1982
Feethams, Darlington
Attendance: 12,557

SHEFFIELD UNITED	DARLINGTON
Waugh	Cuff
Charles	Kamara
Garner	Liddle
Matthews	Smith
MacPhail	Skipper
Kenworthy	Speedie
Morris	McFadden (Stalker)
Trusson	McLean
Edwards	Hawker
Hatton	Wicks
King	Walsh
Manager: Ian Porterfield	Manager: Billy Elliot

Ten years and five days on from the 5-1 demolition of Cardiff, with Woodward, Currie and the rest that had seen United promoted to the top flight, the unthinkable happened. United were a Fourth Division team.

Relegation to the Second Division in 1976 had been a disaster, but then came the first-ever relegation to the third tier. An immediate return looked possible. United were top of the division on Christmas Day, but then keeper Steve Conroy broke his arm, followed by the infamous 4-0 'Boxing Day Massacre' at Hillsborough. The Owls won promotion, United slumped to mid-table and the supporters vowed that the club would 'fight forever more.'

If that was bad, what was to follow in 1980/81 was far worse. United were in the top half of the table for the first half of the season, but another post-Christmas slump followed. By 2 May, when Walsall were the visitors to Bramall Lane, the Saddlers were just a point behind United in the last relegation spot, which meant that United needed a draw to avoid a once-unimaginable relegation to the Fourth Division. With the game scoreless at 85 minutes, Walsall were awarded a penalty, which they converted. Four minutes later, United had a penalty of their own. Don Givens missed, and United were down.

The exciting, swashbuckling side of the early 1970s, with the talismanic Tony Currie bossing the play against the best in the country on a three-sided ground were a distant memory. This was at a time when Sheffielders of any footballing persuasion needed something to lift them more than ever, with the steel and coal industries in terminal decline and unemployment at record levels. Now, though, United were down in the league's basement division.

Changes were made at all levels. The chairman was replaced by businessman Reg Brealey, who quickly poached manager Ian Porterfield from Rotherham. As United had been relegated out of the Third Division, Porterfield had been celebrating winning it with the Millers, but he saw the potential at Bramall Lane and a promise of money to spend was enough to tempt him to drop down two divisions to join the Blades. He made a number of signings, and the club made a massive loss over the season, but fans started to enjoy life again. Winning is always a nice feeling, as are goals, and Porterfield had made a popular signing by bringing former striker Keith Edwards back to the club. Edwards formed a good partnership with Bob Hatton, signed the previous season, and between them they scored 50 of United's 94 in the season, Edwards scoring the lion's share.

The fans also enjoyed visiting grounds that they had never been to before, and deep down they hoped they would never have to go to again. Most clubs in the division had their biggest crowds for years when they hosted United. A 4-0 win over Peterborough (Edwards scoring two) in front of nearly 24,000 at Bramall Lane clinched promotion, so the Blades needed a point away at Darlington the following Saturday to make sure of the league title.

It was United's first-ever league game at Feethams, and Blades supporters travelled up the A1 in vast numbers, with at least 45 coaches and two 'Football Special' trains making the journey.

The official attendance in the record books is 12,557. However, crowd control outside of the ground broke down on the cricket side of the ground behind one of the goals, where the gates were opened, so the official attendance is probably a massive understatement.

To put even that number into context, the previous home game at Darlington had attracted 1,612, and the largest crowd before the United match was in the derby against Hartlepool, 4,575.

Darlington fans may even have stayed away for the day, or they kept themselves to themselves as the Sheffield hordes took over their town and their stadium. The thousands of travelling Blades were determined to enjoy themselves, and the atmosphere was that of a party. After the game, the Durham police commended the Blades fans on their behaviour, in an era when football supporters were making headlines for the wrong reasons.

Fancy dress shops in South Yorkshire must have sold out of all stocks. As *The Star, Sheffield* reporter Tony Pritchett described, 'I saw four gorillas dancing ring-a-roses ... a circus clown embracing Superman and a bishop with his arms around the devil.'

The Darlington team sportingly formed a guard-of-honour as the United players took to the field, wearing the yellow-and-brown striped away kit which, along with the luminous lime-green number from 1989/90, is probably the most affectionately remembered away kit amongst Blades fans.

Darlington had a promising young striker called David Speedie, who would sign for Chelsea two weeks later, and Porterfield had clearly picked him out as the danger man, Paul Garner given the task of marking him out of the game, which he did throughout.

United started on the front foot, determined to finish the season off in style. John Matthews fed a ball through to Hatton, but Smith was alert to the danger, and cleared, and the same defender was on hand when Edwards was in a good position to shoot.

The breakthrough came after 24 minutes, when Edwards, on the right, and Hatton, in the middle, broke through the Darlington line, with Edwards feeding the ball to Hatton to put him one-on-one with Cuff in the Quakers' goal. Hatton finished superbly, sending all four sides of the ground into a mass celebration.

Five minutes later United doubled their lead. A long kick by keeper Keigh Waugh found Edwards, with Kamara in close attendance. After a tussle for the ball, Edwards managed to get a shot away which went just inside the post and rippled the net.

Wigan were the only club that could catch United, but they were losing 2-0 at Aldershot as United led by the same scoreline. With the championship trophy seemingly now on its way to Bramall Lane, the football was now secondary to the party going on around the pitch, as police struggled to keep the surging crowd off the pitch,

Ernest Needham, arguably United's greatest-ever player, at the toss before the 4-4 draw in the 1899 FA Cup semi-final against Liverpool

The 1902 FA Cup winning team – Back row (left-right): Johnson, Thickett, Foulke, Boyle, Wilkinson, Needham. Front row: Barnes, Alf Common, Hedley, Priest, Lipsham

Surrounded by thickening yellow fog, captain George Utley shakes hands with his opponent before the 1915 FA Cup Final at Old Trafford

Billy Gillespie leads the team out at Wembley in the 1925 FA Cup Final

The old Shoreham Street Kop starts to fill up pre-match, 1980s

*The Maestro,
Tony Currie,
September 1973*

Deadly duo Agana and Deane celebrate promotion at Leicester, 1990

'Deano', scorer of the first ever Premier League goal, in action in the game against Manchester United, 1992

A happy St Patrick's Day for Alan Kelly, the hero of the penalty shoot-out against Coventry, 1998

Paul Peschisolido doesn't know what to do with himself after scoring against Forest, 2003

Michael Brown is mobbed after his stunning strike against Wednesday, 2003

Manager Warnock congratulates stand-in keeper Jagielka after a clean sheet against Arsenal, 2006

David Unsworth scores the injury-time winner against Hull, 2006

Blades fans at Wembley celebrate as United lead there for the first time in 89 years, v Hull, 2014

Ryan Flynn scores the winner at Villa Park, 2014

Leon Clarke celebrates his goal with the jubilant Blades away support at Northampton, 2016

The Bouncekiller – Mark Duffy puts United back in front at Hillsborough in 2017

Ollie Norwood congratulations Scott Hogan on scoring United's first goal against Ipswich, 2019

Jack O'Connell heads the ball (not a brick for once) home for United's second against Ipswich, 2019

Two of our own – captain Billy Sharp with manager Chris Wilder

particularly in the cramped covered terrace on the cricket ground end, the sheer numbers making this an almost-impossible task. Many younger fans sat on the track behind the goal line for safety.

Edwards had a good chance to add a third early in the second half. Some great play left Chris Kamara in his wake, but the future Blades defender and Sky Sports presenter managed somehow to get back and put in a challenge as Edwards bore down on goal.

Colin Morris, a mid-season signing from Blackpool who had already become a fan favourite, then went on a good run down the left, putting in one of his trademark accurate crosses to find Charles in space, but the shot was fired over. In the 61st minute, Morris went in full flight again, this time drawing a foul and winning a free kick that Edwards slammed against the bar. The Blades still attacked, roared on by pretty much every member of the crowd, Edwards setting up Matthews, whose shot took a deflection. The ball rolled just wide.

There were no more goals, and it was fitting that Hatton and Edwards were the scorers of the two. Edwards had scored 35 league goals for the season, which is a post-war club record and was enough to win the divisional Golden Boot, while Hatton had contributed another 15 to make a combined total of 50.

'Champions, champions,' chanted the United faithful, as the final whistle came and the fans surged on to the Feetham's turf to celebrate. There would be another party to come a few days later, a friendly against Everton at Bramall Lane for the trophy to be presented.

Who cared if it had only been the Fourth Division? It was United's first silverware for 29 years and, on a sunny day in May, the Blades faithful had reason to celebrate again, and they did so in style.

v Orient 6-3

Football League Third Division
3 March 1984
Bramall Lane
Attendance: 10,031

SHEFFIELD UNITED	ORIENT
Tomlinson	Key
Heffernan	Cornwell
Bolton	Osgood
Arnott	Corbett
Stancliffe	Sussex
Charles (Brazil,60)	Hales
Morris	Silkman
Atkins	Brooks
Edwards	Godfrey
McHale	Kitchen
Garner	McNeil
Manager: Ian Porterfield	Manager: Frank Clark

Please allow me to indulge myself, just for this one game, as this was where it all began for me.

I had been to the Lane before. Mundella School had been given cheap tickets to an England Under-21s match against West Germany two years earlier, but this had been in the Bramall Lane upper tier and in a crowd of just 6,000.

My parents had been regular visitors to Bramall Lane in the early 70s, watching Woodward and Currie, and told tales of visiting players like George Best. My arrival in 1973, and, later, that of my sister, combined with United's decline and increasing crowd trouble, had put paid to that.

Still, I was brought up to love red and white, and to believe that 'typical Wednesdayites' were miserable, pessimistic folk who lived under a delusion of greatness that was always disappointed, while Blades were optimistic, not expecting too much, and capable of enjoying themselves in the most trying of circumstances.

Hooliganism had been the main reason why my mother hadn't wanted me to go, and this was echoed across the country, as attendances dropped sharply. The 1983/84 season saw the lowest average crowd in the First Division since the First World War, below 20,000 for the first time. For context, the 1948/49 season had an average of almost 39,000, and only a decade earlier the average had been over 30,000.

There were still the hardcore who wanted their fix of football, or of violence, or both. School friends who were already going to Bramall Lane were telling tales of the goalscoring exploits of Keith Edwards, and tricky wing play of Colin Morris, and also of the fights on the terraces.

Other kids in the school were, of course, making the longer trek across the city to see Wednesday. There was plenty of interest in the results, as both teams pushed for promotion out of their divisions, Wednesday (successfully) from the second and the Blades from the third in their second season following the 1981/82 promotion. Many a playground fight, physical and verbal, started, especially when the 'Boxing Day massacre' taunts came out, and I wore my replica shirt with pride.

All of this, and I hadn't even been to see them play yet!

My desire to go grew and grew, especially as United pulled off some good early results, a 4-0 opening day win against Gillingham, 5-3 against Scunthorpe, 5-0 against both Southend and Bolton, all before the New Year.

Finally, my parents relented, telling me at Christmas that Dad would take me, and it was now a question of when, not if. Fitting it around my fireman father's shifts, ruling out the Millwall game for obvious reasons, and the vagaries of the fixture list meant that the first available Saturday game that he could take me to was on the first weekend in March, at home to Orient.

What is surprising, looking back, is that I clearly remember being taken aback by the noise of the crowd, and the size, when in fact the stadium was two-thirds empty and Orient brought very few travelling supporters. Still, it was the largest I had seen, the Under-21s game being my only point of reference. The promotion push had clearly not captured the imaginations of the 'floating' fans, who had returned briefly for the culmination of the Fourth Division title-winning campaign.

Some of them had hung on for the start of the next season, but United had never really threatened, and by the penultimate home game of 1982/83, against Bristol Rovers, the support had petered out to a post-war low of 7,694.

Even with the team in the last promotion spot on New Year's Day, three points clear of Dave Bassett's Wimbledon, the casual supporters seemed to be unconvinced, and although a crowd of 22,756 did turn up to the Boxing Day local derby against Rotherham, the previous home league game had attracted less than 10,000.

As if to prove that the public were right to stay away, the first seven games of the New Year brought just one win (in the aforementioned Millwall game). United dropped to sixth, with a five-point gap to Oxford in the third promotion place, who also had two games in hand.

Two wins, away to Brentford on the Saturday before the Orient game, then in the midweek at home to Plymouth, restored some confidence.

Next up were Orient at home. A ten-year-old me walked with my dad through the turnstiles for the Shoreham Street Kop for the first time. I took it all in. The click of the turnstiles, the open-roofed gents' toilet on the right and its pungent aroma, the sloped walk up to the vast terracing, the smell of second-hand Wards Best Bitter, pies and cigarettes as I walked on to the Kop for the first time.

Positioning ourselves towards the front, Dad saw somebody he knew, while I spotted that the kids positioned themselves at the front, so I went to join them. The players came out to warm up, as the tannoy announcer read out the teams, each name being responded to with a ''way' or a 'booo', and then they disappeared back down the tunnel for the final team-talks.

Out they came again, as toilet rolls streamed over the high red fencing and into young keeper Paul Tomlinson's goalmouth.

Tomlinson had just turned 19, and he had broken into the team to replace Keith Waugh earlier in the season, saving a penalty on his debut in the 5-0 win over Southend, and had kept a clean sheet in all eight league games he had played at Bramall Lane.

Orient (who would be 'Leyton Orient' again three years later) were six points behind United, and they had won the Brisbane Road meeting in October 2-0, as well as inflicting a 4-1 defeat on the Blades in the last match of the previous season. They were managed by Frank Clark, a European Cup winner as a player with Forest five years earlier who would go on to manage at the City Ground with some success in the 1990s.

United kicked off, and went immediately on the attack, Edwards bringing the ball down the left and crossing for Morris. After a scramble, the ball was cleared. The same combination attacked again, but the cross from Edwards was too high for the 5ft 6in Morris, then it was Morris's turn to attempt to turn provider from the other flank, the Os' defence scrambling it away again.

United had dominated the first ten minutes and looked much the better team, but Orient then had their first chance to score, Cornwell playing a fine cross-field ball to put McNeil through. Thankfully for United, he lacked composure and scuffed the shot which rolled harmlessly to Tomlinson.

The Orient defenders were having a torrid time of it. Morris sent Kevin Arnott free down the right, and Arnott sent the ball towards the far post. Bob Atkins got his head to it, but the effort towards the opposite post lacked power and, after a slight fumble, Key was able to save it on the ground.

Irish defender Tom Heffernan next sent a ball over the top for Edwards to beat the Orient offside trap. Edwards shot with power, but Key was able to get his hands to it. The ball rebounded to Steve Charles, but at a difficult height, and his effort went wide with an empty goal in front of him.

The second ten minutes had passed with United dominant but unable to convert their chances, but, just like the first ten had done, ended with a good chance for Orient, former Doncaster forward Kitchen evading a challenge from United skipper Paul Stancliffe, but his cross was poor and dealt with by Paul Garner tracking back from midfield.

United seemed to run out of a bit of steam now after a relentless but unrewarded first 20 minutes, and the next 20 passed without much incident. The closing minutes of the half, though, more than made up for this.

In the 40th minute, Charles won the ball on the left to feed Atkins, who played an accurate through-ball to put Edwards through. Although being harassed by Osgood, Edwards had the strength, balance and composure to hold him off and put an accurate shot just inside the post and put United one goal up.

Orient kicked off, but Heffernan was able to immediately win the ball and again played a ball over the heads of the Orient defence to put Edwards through on goal again. He again showed trademark composure, putting the ball past Key to make the score 2-0 to the Blades.

Two minutes later, and Orient got in on the act, Silkman finding space to shoot from 30 yards, his shot accurate, powerful and enough to beat Tomlinson. After 764 minutes, the keeper had finally conceded a league goal at Bramall Lane.

There was even time for a spot of handbags before half-time, after Orient players reacted to a foul on Hales by Charles, before the referee blew his whistle.

Orient kicked off the second half and, as United had done in the first, found themselves with a chance to score in the opening minute, which they took. Brooks put a ball into the box where Cornwell had worked his way into space and put a looping header over the keeper and into the net. Orient were level.

Panic seemed to set in to United now, and the fluid, quality play of the first half had vanished. With ten minutes of the half gone, and the Blades' defence at sea, McNeil latched on to a ball from the right and shot towards goal. Tomlinson pulled off a great save with one hand, but could only deflect it to Kitchen, a few yards out with a simple finish. The net bulged as Kitchen blasted home to put Orient ahead, 3-2.

United pressed for an equaliser, and for a while the Orient defence looked capable of handling them, but they were breached in the 71st minute. Paul Stancliffe headed a corner that beat the keeper, only for Silkman to catch it on the line and concede the penalty. Silkman was booked, but Morris ensured that the punishment fit the crime by putting the penalty away to bring the score level.

Five minutes later, Edwards was put in the clear for what seemed like the umpteenth time in the match, and he completed his hat-trick with another superbly clinical finish. It was his 30th goal of the season in league and cup, and now put United back into the lead, sending the fans in the Kop behind the goal wild, including a ten-year-old boy down at the front.

In the 88th minute, the game was put beyond Orient. As they pressed for an equaliser United caught them on the break, the ball finding Heffernan in space who, like Edwards, finished clinically.

Goals in this game were like buses to Totley, and lo and behold, another came within a minute. Again, Edwards was involved, this time drawing a foul in the box to win another penalty, and Morris once more made no mistake. It was his eighth successful penalty of the season (although he had seen two more saved).

United had won a remarkable game, and this moved them back into third place. The Sheffield public now started to believe. Some 17,916 came to the Lane on the following Tuesday for the six-pointer against Oxford and, although United lost, attendances continued to pick up as the season drew to a close. Edwards continued to bang in the goals, eventually winning the Third Division Golden Boot with 33. Defeats to Wimbledon and Bolton meant that United finished their season sitting in third, but Hull were three points behind them with a game remaining, away to Burnley. There were three sets of supporters at Turf Moor that evening, in a game I was genuinely tempted to include in this book, as hundreds of Blades made the trip to cheer on Burnley. In the end, Hull won 2-0, which brought them level on points and goal difference with United, but the Blades had scored 15 more goals, and this was enough to take them up.

As far as I was concerned, though, it was never in doubt, and as the happy Blades support streamed out of Bramall Lane after the Orient game, a father promised his son, in words never truer, 'It's not like that every week.' But the boy had the Blades bug, and it would never leave him.

v Chester City 6-1
Football League Third Division
17 September 1988
Bramall Lane
Attendance: 8,675

SHEFFIELD UNITED	CHESTER CITY
Benstead	Stewart
Wilder	Glenn
Pike	Woodthorpe
Todd	Hinnigan
Stancliffe	Abel
Smith	Lightfoot (Bennett,60)
Duffield	Jakub
Webster	Barrow
Agana	Benjamin
Deane (Francis,80)	Johnson
Bryson	Newhouse
Manager: Dave Bassett	Manager: Harry McNally

The 1980s were, without doubt, Sheffield United's worst decade as a club.

Coming into the decade on the back of a hammering at Hillsborough, dropping to the Fourth Division, and, after scraping back up to the Second Division, three years of arduous, dull, mid-table football followed. Ian Porterfield was sacked in 1986, having spent money that United didn't really have on 'big-name' players well past their best, such as Peter Withe and Phil Thompson.

The club turned, as clubs often do when there is no money, to youth, even going so far as to promote the youth team manager, Billy McEwan, into the main job. The club were (just about) surviving on a core support of around 8,000 fans, and even two Yorkshire derbies against Leeds in successive seasons could only attract 12,000. The days of 40,000 crowds and Woodward and Currie were, despite being only a decade earlier, a distant memory. It is no exaggeration to say that Sheffield United were a club potentially on its way out of business.

On the first two days in January 1988 United conceded 9 goals, firstly losing 4-1 away at Blackburn and then 5-0 at home to Oldham the following day. The Oldham game was the epitomy of the collective state of depression amongst Blades fans as, at 4-0 down, there were ironic chants of 'we want five' eminating from the Kop. The fans had turned their backs on the team, the manager, and the board. McEwan resigned after the game.

United needed a miracle worker, somebody who could make a team out of virtually nothing, who could wheel and deal and spot bargains that nobody else could see.

Fortunately for them, one became available just nine days later.

Dave Bassett had famously taken the Wimbledon 'Crazy Gang' up from the Fourth to the First Divisions in just four years, and they had finished sixth in the top flight before he was tempted by a move to Watford. He had, though, lasted just six months at Vicarage Road, and was fired with the team bottom of the First Division. The following week, he took the challenge of reviving the sleeping Sheffield United giant.

His first job was to avoid relegation. He took a huge gamble, wheeling and dealing on the transfer market and changing the majority of the starting line-up in the space of a few weeks, including bringing in a classy-looking pacy striker called Tony Agana from Watford, who scored the winning goal against Barnsley on his debut.

Although the football was more exciting, the gamble failed, and United were relegated to the Third Division. Bassett offered his resignation, but the board stuck by him, and he added a few more players to the squad he had built. Striker Francis Joseph, who had played with Bassett at Wimbledon, was brought in, as was a young, gangly striker from Doncaster called Brian Deane. In the first game against Reading, Joseph was partnered with Deane, and scored the second goal in a 3-1 win, but he picked up an injury in the game. Deane also scored in the game, on his debut. Joseph's injury meant that Bassett needed to start Agana and Deane together in the next game. It would be the first time they had started together in a competitive game.

Both of them got on the scoresheet in the game, a 2-2 League Cup draw at Hartlepool, and again in the next league game, a 4-1 win over Bristol Rovers.

United fans needed convincing, though, that Bassett was the man to revive the dying club. Just 9,586 had turned up for the Bristol game, and for this next home game, against Chester, the attendance was under 9,000.

Chester had started the season well, with two wins and a draw from the first three, conceding just one goal in those three games before they travelled to Sheffield.

United, though, dominated the game from the kick-off. Kicking towards the Shoreham Street Kop in the first half, captain Paul Stancliffe went close early on, followed soon after by Ian Bryson, and it looked only a matter of time before the Blades would score.

The goal arrived after just seven minutes. Pike's corner from the right was in the perfect place for Deane, at the far post, to power a header past the Chester keeper.

Chester were a big, strong team, but United were equal to them in every department. Chris Wilder and Martin Pike in the full-back positions bullied their opposite numbers, and Simon Webster was playing a perfect game in the holding-midfielder role.

In the 27th minute, United made it 2-0. Ian Bryson, another pre-season bargain (from Kilmarnock), played a ball into Agana at the edge of the area, who touched it first time to Deane making a diagonal run from the left. Deane's finish was sublime, chipping the ball over the keeper who was trying to narrow the angle, and into the net.

It took Deane just ten minutes more to complete his hat-trick, but it owed much to Wilder's cross from the right, a near-perfect in-swinger at the right height for Deane to meet it at the far post. He had taken just 37 minutes to complete his hat-trick.

United had been outstanding in the first half, and probably should have been five or six goals ahead, but Chester managed to pull one back within ten minutes of the restart, sloppy defending handing Lightfoot a chance which he put away.

Two minutes later, though, City were caught on the break as they chased the game. A long ball was flicked on by Deane for Agana to latch on to in the box. Despite the attentions of a defender, Agana shot home from a tight angle, almost on the byline to the left of the goal.

If Chester were disorganised and outclassed before, now they were totally demoralised as well, and the game was as good as over. With ten minutes to go, Bassett took off Deane. He had scored three, and set up the fourth, and came off to a standing ovation. Bramall Lane already knew what Agana was capable of, but now they were certain they had another gem of a striker.

Deane's replacement was another bargain-basement striker that Bassett had signed in pre-season, John Francis from non-league Emley. Francis had scored the winner in the final of the short-lived Yorkshire & Humberside Cup, against Neil Warnock's Scarborough, and now he made his league debut.

Agana was a quick forward, but Francis was like lightning. As if to prove who was faster, the two raced together with a defender for a ball down the right. Francis was the winner, and he fed Agana to shoot from a similar angle to his first goal. Although the keeper got a slight touch, the ball rolled into the net.

With a minute to go, Francis played a short pass to Agana in midfield. Agana brought the ball forward, finishing well from 15 yards before the centre-half could get his challenge in.

United had scored six, and the scoreline could and should have been even higher. Deane had missed two good chances (the last two of his three were arguably more difficult chances than the two he missed), while winger Peter Duffield also missed what was probably the easiest chance of the half, with the goal at his mercy.

The result sent a message, not only for the rest of division, but also to the Sheffield public. This was the real deal. Three days after the Chester win, a home game against Northampton attracted an additional 3,000, and they were treated to another fine display as the Blades ran out 4-0 winners, with Agana and Deane both scoring again. They would go on to total 59 for the season in league and cup. The partnership would be a huge factor in back-to-back promotions and the two names trip as one off the tongues of Blades fans. Brian Deane and Tony Agana – one of the great Sheffield United strike partnerships, which clicked in front of the lowest crowd of the season, and propelled the Blades back up the divisions. The Blades' revival was underway.

v Brighton & Hove Albion 5-4

Football League Second Division
9 September 1989
Bramall Lane
Attendance: 12,653

SHEFFIELD UNITED	BRIGHTON & HOVE ALBION
Tracey	Keeley
Hill	Chivers
Barnes	Chapman
Booker	Curbishley (Crumplin,82)
Stancliffe	Bissett
Morris	Gatting
Roberts (Whitehouse,70)	Nelson
Gannon	Wood
Francis	Bremner
Deane	Codner
Bryson	Wilkins
Manager: Dave Bassett	Manager: Barry Lloyd

'How are we going to live with that lot?' wrote Matthew Bell in the United fanzine *Flashing Blade* before the season began.

Having won promotion back to the second tier, even surviving in the division looked to be a daunting task. Eleven of the clubs had been in top flight at some point in the last five years, and as well as them a resurgent Leeds under Howard Wilkinson and a Wolves team with momentum after back-to-back promotions. United had gained entry to a tough league.

Thankfully, they had one of the best managers in the business, who knew how to build a team in every sense of the word, and how to spot an absolute bargain.

Two such signings, Brian Deane and Tony Agana had scored 59 goals between them in league and cup in the Third Division promotion campaign, but Deane had no experience in the top two divisions, so there were question marks about whether he could deliver. Any such doubts were destroyed in a barnstorming first game away at West Brom, who were tipped to challenge for promotion. Agana scored a brace and Deane also scored in a 3-0 demolition of the Baggies, which was followed by a 2-0 win at home to Ipswich.

Before the next league game, at Ayresome Park, Agana picked up a back injury. His replacement was another bargain basement signing, the small, but incredibly fast, John Francis, signed from non-league Emley. Francis took just nine minutes to make an impact, somewhat fortunately, but United also conceded their first league goals of the season and, despite being two goals ahead early in the second half, had to settle for a 3-3 draw. Still, against expectations, United were the team asking the questions of their opponents.

Brighton came to Bramall Lane for the fourth game, just a point behind United. The previous season they had been in a relegation scrap, but four 2-1 wins in five games from Easter weekend onwards had proven their battling qualities and pulled them clear.

Just as with the 6-1 win over Chester nearly a year earlier, the Sheffield public had not been tempted by the good start and, as a result, many of them would miss arguably the best game of the season, not just at Bramall Lane, but arguably in the division as a whole.

With Agana still injured, Francis was rewarded for his goal at Middlesbrough with another start, and he returned the favour by providing the assist for the opener. And, just like his goal at Middlesbrough had done, it came after just nine minutes. Ian Bryson's long throw from the left into the area found Francis unmarked at the near post. Despite being the smallest player on the pitch, he had space and time to get his head to the ball and flick it back towards the far post, where Bob Booker had slipped his marker and met the ball on the volley to put the ball past Keeley in the Seagulls' net; 1-0.

Five minutes later the lead was doubled. Bryson again was involved, beating Chivers and chipping the ball into Deane at the near post. Deane glanced a header towards goal which took a deflection off his marker to beat the keeper. It can be argued that it was an own goal, as Deane's header would probably have gone wide, but it mattered little to Deane, or to the Blades fans whose team were now two up after just 14 minutes.

On 31 minutes, full-back David Barnes played a 40-yard free kick from the left wing into the box that swung in as it came down. Again, remarkably, Francis beat the defender in the air, this time with his back to goal, heading it to Deane to his left. Deane miscontrolled it, but this resulted in him accidentally backheeling it back towards Francis, who had turned his man and, as Keeley came out to claim the ball at the near post, slotted home. This time there was nothing lucky about Francis's finish and, after 31 minutes, United were, it seemed, cruising to another victory.

In the summer, manager Dave Bassett had spent almost £400,000 on defenders – Colin Hill, David Barnes and Paul Beesley, which was a relative fortune for the club at the time, but this new-look defence was breached just three minutes after Francis had scored. A long throw from the Brighton left flicked on into the box, and a blocked shot rebounded to winger Paul Wood. His marker, Barnes, was guilty of following the ball instead of the man, and Wood had time to shift the ball on to his left foot, fooling Tracey, and slotting the ball past a diving Morris on the line.

United took a 3-1 lead to half-time, but the defence had shown real cracks. These were exploited again three minutes after the break. Brighton found themselves two-on-one down the left, and Chapman was able to get an early cross in from deep. United had six defenders in the box to deal with Brighton's two attackers, but they stood rooted to the spot as if mesmerised by the quality of the cross. Bremner got up, and he headed home. Brighton had their tails up now, and they pressed for the equaliser.

It came with a similar move to their second, neat play down the left and a deep swinging cross, this time from Codner, was met by a Brighton man in the box. Tracey did well to block the shot, but he could only parry it into the path of Bremner, who just had to poke it home. Four minutes later, Brighton won the ball again in midfield and played it forward. United should have had no problem in clearing, but Hill and Morris both went for the same ball and got in a tangle, resulting in Hill going to ground. Brighton were able to take the ball down a now-undefended left wing.

United still had the numerical advantage, five defenders against two forwards in the box, but Barnes again had allowed Wood acres of space at the back post. From a tight angle on the right, Wood shot towards the far post, and the ball rippled the net. In 34 minutes of play, United had gone from 3-0 up to being a goal behind.

A few moments later, Unitedites were, perhaps, fearing this was not going to be their day, as Deane found himself with a clear chance but, uncharacteristically, skied his effort over the bar from a few yards out.

It was frantic stuff, and now it was the Seagulls' turn to self-destruct at the back. A long ball from the back and again the diminutive Francis beat the centre-half in the air from a standing start, flicking it on before turning his man and bearing down on goal.

It was now a race to the ball between Francis and the onrushing keeper. Francis won the race, just, and was able to touch it past the keeper, who brought down the United forward. Penalty. Up stepped Ian Bryson, who put the ball high to the keeper's right, and levelled the game with 15 minutes to go. The clock ticked down, and it looked like United had rescued a point, but there was more sloppy defending to come, this time from Brighton, who failed to adequately clear a Deane cross.

The ball came to Gannon, who sprayed the ball on to the right wing. Bryson, switched from left to right wing for the last 20 minutes to allow for substitute Dane Whitehouse, now took on, and easily beat, Chapman.

He put an accurate ball into the middle of the box, ten yards from goal, where a diving John Francis met it with his head and just inside the keeper's left-hand post. With a minute to go, United led again. It was, perhaps, the pick of the nine goals, and a fitting way to end the goal-fest.

United had passed their first test and, for all of the money spent on the defence, it had been the low-budget attack that had won the day. As if to prove Bassett's eye for a bargain, none of the four scorers had any experience of the top two English divisions prior to this season. Joining Deane and Francis on the scoresheet were Bob Booker, a free transfer from Brentford who was fast becoming a cult-hero at the Lane, and Ian Bryson, a winger signed from Kilmarnock who would serve United well over the next few seasons.

Brighton's Bremner and Wood had been their stars of the day, and Wood obviously impressed Bassett, as he signed him from Brighton in the second half of the season for £90,000. His first goal for United came in the return fixture, a 2-2 draw at the Goldstone Ground.

The funds for the Wood transfer had come from the sale, two weeks earlier, of John Francis to Burnley for exactly the same fee. Despite his man-of-the-match role in the Brighton game, he was always going to be second-choice behind Agana, and was able to get more regular football with Burnley.

The win took United to the top of the league, a spot that they would hold on to until mid-December, and it would be another six games before the Blades tasted defeat. Even this was a remarkable game where the team lost to West Ham despite having (a possible league record) 28 corners, 23 of which came in the second half.

The crowds started growing as the public started to believe that a second-successive promotion was possible, but, for the second season in a row (after the 6-1 win over Chester in 1988/89), the lowest crowd of the season had been treated to a cracker.

v Leicester City 5-2

Football League Second Division
5 May 1990
Filbert Street, Leicester
Attendance: 21,134

SHEFFIELD UNITED	LEICESTER CITY
Tracey	Hodge (Reid,45)
Hill	Mauchlen (Fitzpatrick,65)
Barnes	Paris
Booker	Ramsey
Wilder	North
Morris	James
Wood (Bradshaw,85)	Mills
Rostron	Oldfield
Agana	Kelly
Deane (Whitehurst,73)	McAllister
Bryson	Wright
Manager: Dave Bassett	Manager: David Pleat

Eighteen months earlier, Bob Booker had been told by Third Division Brentford that he was surplus to requirements. He had invested in a window-cleaning business to prepare for his post-football life. Now, here was a 32-year-old player, soaked in beer, and celebrating promotion to the top flight of English football. If any player epitomised the Sheffield United team at this time, it was Booker. Like the team, he had limited talent, but used what he did have to full effect, and gave it everything he had.

In a cup game at Mansfield in the 1988/89 Third Division promotion season, midfielder Simon Webster had his leg broken. Looking for a quick replacement, Bassett remembered a player who had played for Brentford against the Blades earlier in the season. Booker was signed on a free and came straight into the first team. The wonderfully silly chant 'ooh-aah, Bob Bookah' was soon to be heard at Blades matches, three years before anyone knew who Cantona even was!

Back in the second tier, United had led the division until the Saturday before Christmas, and they were five points clear of third-placed Sunderland as the 1990s began, full of hope for a brighter future for the world with the fall of the iron curtain and for Blades fans with the Bassett revolution. The future seemed to be potentially even sweeter as, across Sheffield, neighbours Wednesday were struggling. They had been 'top dog' in Sheffield for the whole of the 1980s, having returned to the top flight in 1984, under manager Howard Wilkinson before he left for the Leeds job four years later. His replacement was 'Big' Ron Atkinson.

His appointment had not had the desired effect. In November, when the two Sheffield clubs faced each other in the short-lived ZDS Cup, Wednesday were bottom of the First Division while United were top of the Second. United took Wednesday to extra time before losing 3-2.

In January 1990, a TV crew rolled into Bramall Lane to begin filming a BBC2 documentary, imaginatively titled *United*. The arrival of the production crew marked a downturn in form, which probably had much to do with the exertions of an FA Cup run to the quarter-finals which involved nine games. Five league games were lost after the cup run, most crucially the Easter Monday 4-0 defeat at leaders Leeds, which saw United drop out of the automatic promotion places for the first time since September. Newcastle had overtaken them with just four games remaining. Across the city, Wednesday had undergone a revival. By the end of March they were nine points clear of the relegation places. The Blades fans' ultimate dream of swapping places was dissolving.

The Saturday after the Leeds defeat, the Blades reclaimed second spot with a Brian Deane winner against Port Vale with the last kick of the game. Wednesday, meanwhile, had slipped again and were now just three points ahead of Luton in the last remaining relegation spot.

Three games remained for United. A 4-2 win over relegation battlers Bournemouth and a goalless draw at Blackburn meant that everything came down to the last day. United needed a victory or, if they did not, hoped that Newcastle also failed to win. In the division above, Wednesday needed a point at home to Forest to secure their top-flight status, or hoped that Luton did not win at Derby.

Some 10,000 Blades fans travelled to Leicester on a sunny first Saturday in May. Leicester had allocated a good portion of the ground to the travelling support. The crowd was virtually an even-split between Leicester and Blades supporters. Long-serving club captain Paul Stancliffe had been injured in the Port Vale game, so

Bob Booker led the team out, resplendent in the luminous lime-green away kit and red shorts which seemed to glow brighter in the May sunshine.

Leicester started the more lively of the two teams. Gary McAllister went close with a free kick then Tony James headed just over from a corner before a poor clearance from Mark Morris set up Gary Mills to hit home a half-volley after seven minutes and put the Foxes into the lead. Bassett later admitted that he 'started to fear the worst,' but that the players 'took the game by the scruff of the neck and subjected Leicester to intense pressure.'

Ian Bryson, attacking down the left, picked out Paul Wood's run with a lovely ball into the box, and Wood scored with a brave diving header. The lead had lasted just eight minutes.

Seven minutes later, an almighty goalmouth scramble saw former Wednesday goalkeeper Martin Hodge pull off a double save, then two shots were cleared off the line before the ball landed at the feet of Deane who could not miss from a yard out. During the scramble, Martin Hodge had taken an accidental knee to the face, and required lengthy treatment. Still dazed, he resumed, but poor Leicester defending and United's high pressing didn't help his cause. Agana was able to volley home from Deane's flick-on in the 36th minute, then Wilf Rostron's long-range effort bobbled home four minutes later. Leicester's Marc North had started the game in defence, gone into goal when Hodge was receiving treatment, and was now moved up front by manager Pleat. With a minute remaining in the half, he reacted quickest in the United area when the defence failed to deal with a long throw from James, to add Leicester's second.

After a wonderful, crazy half, things were looking good for United, despite mass confusion in the dressing room between Bassett and assistant manager Geoff Taylor over who should be standing where when defending a corner, comedically captured on the cameras for the documentary. To this day, nobody is really sure if it was Wilf (Rostron) or Jock (Ian Bryson) that was meant to be the zone man, but United did not concede from a corner in the second half, so something went right!

The second half was less eventful. Hodge was unable to resume for Leicester after half-time, so North had gone back in goal.

Leicester attacked half-heartedly, but Booker led the line well and Tracey commanded his area.

At one point, Booker brought down Leicester midfielder Gary McAllister, who was valued at over £1m and had already attracted a bid from Brian Clough's Forest. 'Ooh-aah, Bob Bookah,' sang the Blades.

As he got up, McAllister screamed at Booker, 'Who the hell are you?'

'I'm Ooh-ahh Bob Bookah.' came the reply. 'Can't you hear them?' With their team two goals ahead, United fans in the ground were busy celebrating while at the same time listening for news from elsewhere on their radios. The Newcastle result was looking more and more irrelevant, but they were losing at Middlesbrough anyway, while Leeds were being held at Bournemouth. If results stayed this way, United would go up as champions.

In the top flight, Luton had come back from two down at Derby to level the game, while Wednesday were a goal down to Forest. Pearce scored his and Forest's second on 64 minutes. Most United fans now prayed for a Luton winner.

It came on 75 minutes through Kingsley Black, while on 82 minutes Nigel Jemson made sure Wednesday would lose by putting Forest 3-0 up. In exactly the same minute of play at Leicester, Paris miscontrolled at the back, leaving an alert Tony Agana one-on-one with the stand-in keeper. Agana touched the ball past him, and it rolled slowly into the net.

The final whistle came, and a mass of Blades fans run on to the pitch to celebrate with their heroes and carry Bassett aloft on their shoulders then taking items of his clothing as souvenirs, leaving him in just his underpants.

The only result that had not gone in United's favour was the Leeds one, as they had scored a later winner at Bournemouth to clinch the title on goal difference. It mattered little to the Unitedites. Bassett's two-and-a-half seasons had seen a relegation followed by two promotions. These were interesting times indeed, and, as he later admitted, confirmed his reputation as 'shit-or-bust Bassett'.

'BLADES GLORY – OWLS DOWN' read the headline in the *Star Green 'Un* by the time the fans had got back to Sheffield. A decade of hurt had been erased on a beautiful May afternoon. United were a First Division team again, above the Owls for the first time in over a decade and, instead of cleaning windows, Bob Booker was now a top-flight footballer.

v Sheffield Wednesday 3-1
Football League First Division
11 March 1992
Hillsborough
Attendance: 40,372

SHEFFIELD UNITED	SHEFFIELD WEDNESDAY
Tracey	Woods
Gage	Nilsson
Barnes	King
Gannon	Palmer
Gayle	Anderson
Beesley	Shirtliff
Bradshaw	Wilson (Jemson,69)
Rogers	Hyde
Davison (Cork,80)	Hirst
Deane	Williams
Whitehouse (Hodges,64)	Pearson (Harkes,72)
Manager: Dave Bassett	Manager: Trevor Francis

Having been relegated from the top flight as United were promoted in the opposite direction on the same day in 1990, Wednesday made an immediate return the following season.

They were, perhaps, a little fortunate that there was an additional automatic promotion place up for grabs, as the top flight was being expanded back to 22 teams, finishing third which would have meant a play-off place in the previous season when United had battled to finish second.

That said, they had proved their mettle by winning the League Cup against Manchester United, to date the only major trophy to be won by either Sheffield club since 1935. Manager Ron Atkinson, though, was tempted away by Aston Villa, so Wednesday promoted Trevor Francis to a player-manager role as his replacement. While the Owls were fighting their way back, United performed a miracle escape on a shoestring budget. Their first league win didn't come until three days before Christmas, but the team went on a great run, winning 12 of the next 18, including a run of 7 wins in a row, and they were safe with four games remaining.

The gulf in resources between the two clubs, with boardroom shenanigans constantly ongoing at Bramall Lane, was evident in the transfer dealings of the two clubs. The Owls net spend for the

1991/92 season was almost £2.7m, including England international keeper Chris Woods, while the Blades made a slight profit in their dealings. Their biggest signing was new captain, defender Brian Gayle, and even then, the transfer was delayed as United couldn't find the funds, manager Dave Bassett actually loaning the club money until it was sorted out.

Both sets of supporters looked forward to the derbies, but arguably the Wednesday fans were relishing it more, given the resources, and also given the start to the season that both clubs, particularly United, had. The message that Wednesdayites gave to their Blades mates was clear. All they needed to do was turn up to each game, and they were going to destroy United.

This is really the tale of two games. When the first top-flight meeting between the two teams in 24 years finally came around, in the November at Bramall Lane, United were rooted to the bottom of the league with just two wins in 15 and six points adrift of safety. The Owls, meanwhile, were flying high in fourth place, six points off the top. Worse still for United, their best player, striker Brian Deane, had only played five games all season (scoring four goals in those) and none for two months, due to glandular fever.

At Bramall Lane, a less-than-100-per-cent-fit Deane was selected, and fears of Wednesday dominating the game weren't helped when Palmer hit a shot against the bar and then Anderson had a goal ruled out for offside. United came back, though, Woods heading off the line, and then, shortly before half-time, they got a real break. A collision in midfield between Sheridan and Warhurst allowed John Gannon to put Ian Bryson one-on-one with the keeper. Woods parried his shot, but the ball fell to Dane Whitehouse, who slotted home to send the Blades behind the goal into a frenzy as he ran to celebrate with them. Whitehouse, who had turned 21 the previous month, was Sheffield-born and a childhood Blades fan. He had established himself as a regular choice over the previous month, and this was just his third league goal for the club.

Danny Wilson, who would later manage both teams, hit the post in the second half for Wednesday but, at the other end, a corner found its way to Deane six yards out. Deane turned beautifully, and his shot rolled through Woods's legs and in for United's second. Whitehouse could have added another before the end, his shot cleared off the line by King. Although the Owls had their chances in the game, United deserved their win, having played with typical Bassett-style passion and intensity throughout.

There was still, though, the return match to think about, which was scheduled for a Wednesday night in March. United's form improved following the Bramall Lane win, and they had climbed out of the relegation zone by the time of the Hillsborough meeting. Wednesday, though, had lost only two games in the 15 league fixtures between the two games and had only lost one game at home, the opening match of the season to Ron Atkinson's Villa.

Wednesday fans went into the game confident of revenge.

On a horribly wet and windy night, a crowd of over 40,000 (the last time to date that a match in Sheffield would exceed this number as the Hillsborough Kop was seated a year later) welcomed Derek Dooley on to the field. This was the first time that Dooley, Wednesday's greatest-ever goalscorer, had been at Hillsborough since they had fired him as manager on Christmas Eve 1973. The following year, he began a 32-year association with the Blades which ended with him being made a lifetime vice-president of the club. Both sets of supporters gave him an emotional standing ovation.

Niceties over, it was time for battle to resume. United were in yellow away shirts, just as Wednesday had been at the Lane, and United fans launched hundreds of matching yellow balloons around the two tiers of the Leppings Lane end. Striker Bobby Davison had been brought in from Leeds on loan, and he was thrown straight into the side. Owls manager Francis had decided to abandon the system that had put them into the top three, perhaps with memories of the Bramall Lane defeat in his mind, by switching to three central defenders.

Perhaps adapting to this change was why Blades midfielder Paul Rogers was able to bisect two defenders with a pass to Deane in the box, and also why Whitehouse was able to so easily slip his marker to Deane's left. Deane cut back the ball from the byline, leaving Whitehouse with a simple tap-in into the empty net from four yards out. If it was the fault of an untried system, it mattered not to Whitehouse, or the thousands of Blades behind the goal. Four minutes gone, and 1-0 up at Hillsborough.

Wednesday attacked, winning a corner that resulted in an almightly scramble which was eventually cleared by the Blades. A superb tackle by Paul Beesley in the United area then prevented Wednesday's top scorer Hirst from getting a shot away as the Owls pressed for a leveller.

United countered. Carl Bradshaw, another childhood Blades fan (and ex-Wednesday player) found himself with space to run down the right. Looking up, he saw Davison making a run into the box, and launched a long pass in front of the loanee. Woods, seeing the run and the pass, came out to collect it. It should have been an easy take for Woods, but he paused slightly, took his eye off the ball and fumbled it straight into the path of Davison. Davison had both Deane and an unmarked Whitehouse to his left in space, but his striker's instinct meant he only had one thing on his mind, and he fired into the net before Pearson could block it. Just 28 minutes gone, and United were two up.

They commanded the rest of the half, with Brian Gayle in particular looking unbeatable at the back, and, late in the half, a deep cross from Davison caused problems but ultimately came to nothing.

As United had done four minutes into the first half, Wednesday then scored four minutes into the second. Whitehouse and Palmer tussled for the ball at the edge of the United area and the referee felt that the young Blade was a little too physical, although it looked a harsh decision as both players seemed guilty of the same thing. Three Wednesday players stood over the ball at the edge of the area on the right for the free kick, the ball was rolled into the path of Phil King, running through the middle, who shot from distance. The ball took a deflection, sending keeper Simon Tracey the wrong way, and into the goal. Wednesday started to dominate now, Wilson orchestrating the play from the middle, but United were well organised and hard to break down. They had a good chance to increase the lead when Beesley headed over from ten yards from a John Gannon cross, but a third goal in the 66th minute really knocked the stuffing out of their rivals.

Gannon, picking up a Kevin Gage throw on the right, played the ball into the box from 40 yards, where Deane and Davison were waiting with the three central defenders. The ball dropped at the right height for Davison to fling himself forward and meet it with his head while the defenders stood and watched. He glanced the ball just inside a flailing Woods's post.

On his Blades debut, in a Sheffield derby at Hillsborough, he had scored twice and written himself into club folklore.

United could have made it four, when Bradshaw's low shot went through Woods's legs but failed to make it into the goal.

Davison was brought off to an ovation by the jubilant Blades, who were singing 'lets all laugh at Wednesday' and dancing around the away end. His replacement was another debutant, Alan Cork, another player who would be fondly remembered by Blades fans in the future.

If Woods and the Wednesday defence were having a stinker, this was compounded in the last minute by Tracey pulling off a brilliant save when Jemson found himself through on goal. Woods had cost Wednesday £1.2m, while Tracey had cost United £12,000, and many on the night were left scratching their heads on why Woods was the one who was being picked for the England squad.

United had, against all expectation, completed the league double against Wednesday, the first since 1962. Winning six of their remaining fixtures, they clawed their way up to a finish of ninth in the table which they have not bettered since. Going into the last game of the season, Wednesday were five points behind Leeds. Had the derbies gone their way, they would have gone into the last game, at home to Liverpool, with a chance to win the league. United had made sure that wasn't going to happen on their watch.

v Manchester United 2-1

FA Premier League
15 August 1992
Bramall Lane
Attendance: 28,070

SHEFFIELD UNITED	MANCHESTER UNITED
Tracey	Schmeichel
Barnes	Irwin
McLeary	Bruce
Beesley	Pallister
Gage	Blackmore
Lake	Ferguson
Bradshaw	Ince (Phelan,7)
Gannon (Hartfield,86)	Kanchelskis (Dublin,68)
Hodges (Bryson,68)	Giggs
Deane	McClair
Cork	Hughes
Manager: Dave Bassett	Manager: Alex Ferguson

There had been talk of a breakaway 'super league' for several years, as the top clubs looked to cash in on the increasing popularity of the sport after the game's low point of the early-to-mid 1980s. The FA saw it as a way to weaken their rival organisation, the Football League, and the top clubs saw a way to increase their incomes.

At the time, it seemed timely for United. The Dave Bassett revival had seen them return to the First Division at last and then survive two relegation battles to stay there. Along with the other 21 clubs in the top flight, at the end of the 1991/92 season they resigned from the Football League and became founder members of the Premier League.

It was, and felt like, a new era, for better or worse, and United fans took pride in Carl Bradshaw's inclusion in the 'Alive and Kicking' Sky Sports advertising campaign. The new league had signed an unprecedented TV rights deal with Sky and the BBC, valued at over £300m, and there were several transfers of over £2m in the preceding summer, most notably the British record transfer of Alan Shearer to Blackburn from Southampton for £3.4m.

United, though, continued to operate on a shoestring, as the new-found wealth disappeared into a black hole of debt and poor housekeeping by the board. While clubs spent millions on players, the Blades' only signing was reserve keeper Alan Kelly from Preston for £150,000, although this would turn out to be an inspired purchase. With defenders Colin Hill and Chris Wilder being sold, United turned a £100,000 transfer profit in the pre-season. A huge contrast, then, to opening day visitors Manchester United, who had just missed out on the title the previous season and were expected to challenge again. Their starting line-up had cost over £10m in total, compared with the Blades' £1.1m. The only debutant for the Blades on the day was loanee from First Division Millwall, Alan McLeary.

'We know that we can't compete with big transfers,' said Bassett. 'Four years ago, we were playing in the Third Division. We have made huge strides, but we are trying to catch up.'

Ferguson's team, then, went into the game as strong favourites to begin their assault on the league with a win. Games between the two teams at Bramall Lane had, in recent years though, been tight affairs, with just one goal separating the teams in the last three meetings in cup and league (the Blades winning the home league meeting in 1990/91).

Other big changes had taken place over the summer, including a substitute keeper (although only two subs could be used) as well as the back-pass rule, which meant that the goalkeeper could no longer pick up a pass directly from one of his own players. Several pundits and managers, Bassett amongst them, predicted chaos.

The previous two seasons had seen United escape relegation after being in the bottom three at New Year, so Bassett had organised an early Christmas party to try to kick-start the season. The match programme cover featured Bassett dressed as Santa on the Bramall Lane pitch with club captain Brian Gayle and top striker Brian Deane decked out in tinsel, party hats and balloons.

Nine games in the Premier League kicked off at 3pm on the inaugural Saturday, with two held back for live broadcast on the Sunday and Monday, and the stage was set for, on a sunny August afternoon at Bramall Lane, history to be made.

The game started out in combative style, with midfielder Paul Ince going in recklessly against keeper Simon Tracey in the opening minute. Ince came off the worst, though, and, although this probably saved him from getting booked, he had to be substituted soon after.

Tracey was then called into action to deal with a back-pass, under pressure from an onrushing Kanchelskis. Tracey launched the ball forward, Alan Cork flicked the header and Pallister, under pressure from Deane, put the ball out of play, level with the Manchester United area at the Shoreham Street end. Carl Bradshaw launched the throw long to the near post. The ball flicked off a defender's head and straight into the path of an onrushing Brian Deane, who powered a header into the net. Five minutes had gone, the Blades led, and, more significantly, Deane had scored the first-ever goal in the new Premier League. Chants of 'Deano, Deano' echoed around Bramall Lane.

An almost identical build-up two minutes later, Tracey's kick finding Cork's head, sent Deane clear and one-on-one with Schmeichel. His finish was superb, but the assistant referee (or maybe they were still linesmen then) had his flag up, and the goal was disallowed. This was quickly followed by action in the Blades' penalty area. Tracey was forced to make two good saves in succession against Giggs, then Beesley was called upon to cut out a dangerous ball across the box from Kanchelskis.

In the 19th minute, Darren Ferguson, in the middle of the park, played a long ball over the top where Giggs beat the offside trap. Tracey rushed out to meet him, leading with his feet, and cleaned him out. Even the most biased Blade would have to admit that a penalty should have been awarded (and Tracey then sent off for the professional foul). Referee Hill, though, was a long way away, having struggled to keep up with the long ball forward, and nothing was given, despite the vociferous protests from the Manchester players.

They had further reason to feel hard done by two minutes later, when a Giggs shot took a clear deflection off Kevin Gage, but the referee awarded a goal kick instead of a corner.

A Hughes volley from a Giggs cross was put over the bar, then at the other end a cross from deep by Deane caused problems which resulted in a Blades corner. Moments later, Deane was back in defence, winning the ball from Kanchelskis. In front of the England manager, Graham Taylor, Deane was showing off his full range of abilities.

In the 33rd minute, it was Man Utd's turn to have a goal disallowed. Giggs put a high, looping cross in from the right which bounced high and into the goal, but Kanchelskis had clearly bundled Tracey to the ground.

From the resulting free kick came a moment of comedy which almost resulted in a second goal for the Blades. Again, Tracey's kick found the head of Cork. The flick-on found its way to Pallister, but, under pressure, he attempted to head it back to Schmeichel. The keeper was wrong-footed, the ball rolled past him towards the goal, but hit the post, and Schmeichel was able to smother it. Half-time came, and, after an eventful first half the Blades led 1-0.

The second half would start with the same intensity as the first, and within four minutes the Blades were awarded a penalty. A loose ball from Kanchelskis was picked up by John Gannon in the Blades' half, and he played a quick ball forward towards Deane to launch a counter-attack. The ball went past Deane, but defender Bruce decided to go with the man rather than the ball, leaving Cork in the clear and bearing down on goal. Pallister, with a last-ditch challenge, brought him down just as he got into the area.

Deane took the penalty, low to Schmeichel's right, and into the net. Not only had he scored the first goal in the Premier League, he had now taken, and scored, the first penalty. The Blades led 2-0 and tongue-in-cheek chants of 'we're going to win the league' rang around Bramall Lane. The tackles were flying in, Gannon picking up a booking for one on Irwin, then Blackmore put in one on Bradshaw that certainly looked two-footed, but was punished by nothing more than a free kick.

In the 61st minute, Manchester United pulled a goal back, seemingly out of nothing. A long kick from Schmeichel was miscontrolled by McLeary, under pressure from Hughes on the edge of Tracey's area. Hughes was somehow able to wrap his foot around the ball and send a shot towards goal which beat the keeper and rolled into the bottom corner.

'That certainly was route one with a vengeance,' said commentator Barry Davies on the *Match of the Day* highlights later that evening, alluding to the criticisms of the Bassett style of play, 'and not by Sheffield United but by Manchester United'. Ferguson threw on new signing, striker Dion Dublin, in place of Kanchelskis, for the last 20 minutes, as his team threw everything at the Blades looking for an equaliser. Cork gave away a needless foul in the Sheff

Utd half, and a deep cross from Irwin found its way to Dublin on the left. His shot, though, would probably have hit the post had Tracey not smothered it.

The Blades were hanging on to their single-goal lead, and reducing the visitors to long-range efforts. Ferguson, Pallister and Phelan all took turns in trying their luck from outside the area, the first and last well wide, the second straight at Tracey.

Gannon was forced to limp off with two minutes remaining, requiring stiches in his leg, and this proved to be the last significant action of the game, and, as Tracey hit a goal kick high and long, the referee blew for full time.

The Blades had won on their Premier League debut, against a team that would win the league that season and dominate the competition for the next two decades under Ferguson. Brian Deane had written his name in the history books as the scorer of the first-ever goal and the first-ever penalty in the new league. He would be the club's top scorer for the fifth successive season, and he would win a third England cap in the September after this game.

Ferguson, who would build a reputation for giving referees a hard time, criticised the penalty decision, probably rightly, but Bassett retorted, 'I can understand Manchester's disappointment because when we played them at Old Trafford last year, we had two clear penalty claims turned down.'

Only four teams won on that opening day. As well as the Blades, Norwich, Leeds and Coventry were the other three. All four of the winners would spend the majority of the next two decades outside of the Premier League, and all have had spells in the third tier. The United board, in their infinite wisdom, would sell Deane, without Bassett's approval, at the end of the season, and this would result in relegation out of the contest that they had scored the first goal in. The club would return for just one season in the next quarter of a century but, for one glorious sunny August day in 1992, they were the Premier League history makers.

v **Blackburn Rovers** 2-2 (AET)

(Penalties 5-3)
FA Cup Sixth Round Replay
16 March 1993
Bramall Lane
Attendance: 23.920

SHEFFIELD UNITED	BLACKBURN ROVERS
Kelly	Mimms
Gage (Ward,64)	May
Whitehouse	Dobson
Hoyland	Sherwood
Gayle	Hendry
Pemberton	Moran
Littlejohn	Ripley
Hartfield	Marker
Bryson (Beesley,45)	Livingstone (Wegerle,112)
Cork	Wilcox
Hodges	Atkins
Manager: Dave Bassett	Manager: Kenny Dalglish

Dave Bassett's battling Blades had shown some success in cup competitions, reaching the fifth and sixth rounds in his first two full seasons, but the club had not reached a semi-final for over 30 years, and had not been to Wembley since 1936.

At home to Burnley in the third round, this looked like a stretch that would continue. Burnley, sitting in mid-table in the third tier, came to Bramall Lane and took a 2-0 lead which they held until a frantic final ten minutes. United pulled a goal back, a player from each team was sent off for fighting (future Blades manager Adrian Heath, who had scored both Burnley goals, and Adrian Littlejohn for United) and, finally, Paul Beesley scored a last-gasp equaliser to prevent a giant-killing.

This sparked a cup run that provided a welcome distraction from the annual relegation scrap that United were once again embroiled in. In the replay at Turf Moor, Heath put Burnley in the lead again, but within 11 minutes of this United were ahead, and they ran out 4-2 winners, including a Brian Deane hat-trick.

After beating Hartlepool 1-0 at Bramall Lane, the fifth round draw pitted United against league leaders Manchester United, which would be the first-ever match broadcast live from Bramall Lane on free-to-air TV. After the Red Devils took a first-half lead through Ryan Giggs after 30 minutes, the game was turned on its head by half-time. Firstly, Jamie Hoyland managed to bundle a Glyn Hodges free kick over the line, then Hodges himself provided a piece of magic as he lobbed Schmeichel to make it 2-1. Steve Bruce missed a second-half penalty, and the Blades hung on, and they were in the quarter-finals.

Their opponents would be Blackburn, to be played at Ewood Park. Although this was Rovers's first season back in the top flight in 26 years, they had money that United fans could only dream of thanks to millionaire owner Jack Walker, and they had broken the British transfer record by signing Alan Shearer for £3.4m.

Despite their new-found wealth, only 6,721 turned up to Ewood Park, almost half of whom were travelling Blades fans. Four days earlier, United had thrashed Tottenham 6-0 at Bramall Lane, but Blackburn away proved a tougher nut to crack, but they limited Rovers to long-range efforts and secured a 0-0 draw.

Blackburn had progressed to the semi-final of the League Cup too, and, on the Sunday before the Bramall Lane replay, were knocked out by Wednesday, which meant that they were facing the possibility of being knocked out of the cups by both Sheffield teams within the space of three days.

Wednesday had also made progress in the FA Cup, and they had drawn 3-3 against Derby at the Baseball Ground. The cup draw was made, and this set up the prospect of an all-Sheffield semi-final, if both teams won their replays.

United's game was first, on the Tuesday night. Both teams were without their star strikers, Deane and Shearer. Chances were at a premium in the opening exchanges, and United missed Deane's finishing ability in the first real opening, May's poor header across the box was seized upon by Littlejohn, but he showed a lack of composure and volleyed it over the bar.

A sweeping cross-field ball from Pemberton set the pacy Littlejohn free down the right flank. He cut inside and shot, pulling off a good one-handed save from Mimms in front of the United Kop.

They were the best chances of the first half, Blackburn being restricted to a speculative effort from Livingstone that was dealt with by Alan Kelly. United were dealt a blow as Ian Bryson was forced to come off at half-time with a groin injury.

The two teams had played out 135 minutes without a goal, but it took just two minutes of the second half for the deadlock to be broken, and it was Blackburn that took the lead. Wilcox's corner from the right was met by an unmarked Livingstone at the far post, who powered a header into the ground that bounced into the United net.

Littlejohn had another chance that he missed, and then Sherwood hit a beauty, which had Kelly beat but not the woodwork. Another goal would probably have put the tie beyond the Blades.

With 25 minutes remaining, manager Bassett made changes. Mitch Ward, a 21-year-old Sheffield-born utility player, came off the bench in place of Kevin Gage to bolster the attack, and, with less than ten minutes to go, he had levelled the game. Hodges crossed from deep on the left, to find veteran striker Alan Cork at the far post. Under pressure, Cork was only able to head against the back of a defender, but the ball fell kindly for Ward running into the middle to bundle the ball in from close range and take the match to extra time.

Nine minutes into the first half of extra time, Blackburn took the lead again, United's tired defence failing to deal with a run into the the box, and Sherwood was able to put a ball across the box to leave Newell with a simple finish.

United dug deep, and they pushed for another equaliser. It came six minutes into the second period of extra time. Alan Cork made a run to meet a long ball from Beesley at the byline on the left, catching the Blackburn defenders napping and hitting a first-time low cross to the near post. There, again, was Ward to tap home. The same combination, Cork with the assist and Ward with the finish, and United were back in the tie.

The game went to penalties. United had only been awarded one penalty in the last 99 games in all competitions (in the opening game of the season against Manchester United), so were definitely lacking in real-life practice when it came to spot-kicks. After a long wait to get the shoot-out started, Mitch Ward picked up the ball and carried it towards the penalty spot at the Bramall Lane end, in front of the travelling Blackburn supporters.

Ward took a long run-up, and confidently hit the ball into the top left-hand corner to complete a hat-trick of sorts.

Wilcox now stepped up for Blackburn. His penalty was weak, low, and Kelly went the right way to keep it out. Next up was Charlie Hartfield, who took a shorter run-up, five steps, before drilling a low penalty to Mimms's right and into the net. Blackburn captain Hendry scored for Blackburn to make it 2-1, and Alan Cork now walked up to take United's third.

Cork had vowed not to shave until the cup run was ended so was sporting a bushy beard. He was also conspicuous by the lack of hair on his head, leading to the infectious chant 'Alan Cork, Alan Cork, Alan, Alan Cork. He's got no hair, but we don't care, Alan, Alan Cork' by the Blades fans. He placed the ball deliberately and slowly on the spot, took a few steps back, and put it in the same place as Hartfield. Mimms dived the wrong way and the ball flew into the goal.

Wegerle, who had been surprisingly left on the bench until extra time, scored for Blackburn, despite the deafening whistles from the United fans designed to put the Rovers takers off, then Hodges powered an unstoppable left-foot penalty into the Blackburn net. Newell now had to score, but he did so, to make it 4-3 with one each left to take.

The responsibility for United's last penalty was taken by John Pemberton. Bassett, the players and the supporters could barely stand to watch as 'Pembo' began his run-up from the edge of the area. He powered the shot straight and high and past Mimms into the net.

Pemberton had played for Crystal Palace in the 1990 semi-final against Liverpool, which Palace had won after a replay. Manager that day had also been Kenny Dalglish, leading Pemberton to remark that he 'must think I have some sort of a cup hoodoo on him' and that he had felt 'absolutely confident' about the penalty.

Despite never leading in the tie, United had made it to the FA Cup semi-final. 'To say we don't get penalties,' said Bassett, 'or even practice them, they weren't bad ones, were they?'

Blackburn had been knocked out of two cups in three days by Sheffield teams. Now it was down to Wednesday to set up the all-Sheffield semi, which they did by beating Derby 1-0 at Hillsborough the following night.

After a campaign by Sheffield fans to have the game played at the famous stadium, Blades fans travelled to London for the club's first visit to Wembley in almost 60 years. Despite taking Wednesday to extra time, they would succumb to a Mark Bright header in injury time on a memorable day where Alan Kelly performed heroics in the United net after Cork had equalised Waddle's long-range free kick. Wednesday had reached both FA Cup and League Cup finals, but they lost both to Arsenal.

Although United were still involved in a relegation fight, they would survive with a game to spare, beating Forest 2-0 at the City Ground to send them down instead, in Brian Clough's last home game. But the cup run to the semi-final was the real highlight of the season, and the Blackburn epic will never be forgotten by those who stayed past ten o'clock at Bramall Lane that night.

v Sunderland 2-0

38

Nationwide Football League First Division
10 August 1997
Bramall Lane
Attendance: 17,324

SHEFFIELD UNITED	SUNDERLAND
Tracey	Perez
Borbokis	Makin
Quinn (Nilssen,77)	Scott
McGrath	Clark
Tiler	Ball (Bridges,45)
Holdsworth	Melville
Patterson	Agnew
Marker	Ord
Fjortoft (Katchouro,59)	Quinn
Deane	Rae (Byrne,71)
Whitehouse	Gray
Manager: Nigel Spackman	Manager: Peter Reid

There were very few dull seasons for the Blades in the 1990s.

Promotion to the top flight, annual post-Christmas battles against relegation, a first cup semi-final in 32 years at Wembley against Wednesday, a last-minute relegation in 1994 – and that was just the first five seasons of the decade.

After years of boardroom wranglings and selling off their best players, what appeared to be a saviour had arrived, in the shape of DIY tycoon Mike McDonald.

Bassett resigned having been unsuccessful in his attempts to get United back into the Premier League and was replaced with a 'big-name' manager in Howard Kendall, who had won two league championships and an FA Cup with Everton in the 1980s.

At last, a United boss was given money to spend, including the club's first two £1m signings in Don Hutchison and John Ebbrell, plus Norwegian striker Jan-Aage Fjortoft, who made an immediate impact, scoring eight goals in his first nine games. The Ebbrell transfer was less successful, as he unfortunately played for just 45 minutes before picking up an injury that eventually forced his retirement from the game.

In his first full season, Kendall took United into the play-offs, although, given the resources, this was arguably an underachievement. Making the Wembley final, they lost to a last-minute wonder goal by Palace's David Hopkin. Kendall then surprised everyone by resigning to return to 'his' Everton for a third spell as manager. Midfielder Nigel Spackman took over, initially as caretaker-manager but he was confirmed permanent the week before the start of the season.

Kendall had been involved in transfer negotiations before leaving, and Spackman pressed on with these, and added some signings of his own. Two players, Vas Borbokis and Tri Dellas, arrived as unknown quantities from Greece, where Kendall had connections, having managed Xanthi a few years earlier. Defender Paul McGrath also joined, on a rolling contract, as did Nicky Marker, a midfielder from Blackburn, but the signing that created the most excitement amongst Blades supporters was the return of Brian Deane, for £1.5m from Leeds.

The bright August sunshine matched the optimistic mood of the Uniedites as the season began. They had been made to wait an extra day to see the return of 'Deano', as the game against Sunderland had been moved to the Sunday for Sky TV to show live.

The Mackems were expected to challenge for promotion, having been relegated on the last day of the previous season when other results had all gone against them. They had kept faith with manager Peter Reid, who had got them up there in the first place, and he had managed them to victories against Manchester United and Arsenal during the season. Their squad had been left intact.

United's line-up sprung a few surprises. Firstly, the system was a 3-5-2, the wing-backs both being debutants, Borbokis on the right and, on the left, Wayne Quinn, a youth product who had been in the reserves for four years but had impressed Spackman in pre-season friendlies.

McGrath slotted in between Carl Tiler and David Holdsworth the centre-half partnership from the Kendall team, to form the back three, while Marker also made his debut.

The fans, though, were interested in one player. 'Deano, Deano' rang around the stadium as the players warmed up. 'It brought a lump to my throat when we came out,' he said later.

It was Vas Borbokis, though, that really got the crowd going when the game kicked off, with a nice run from the right before testing Perez in the Sunderland goal. He followed this up by trapping the ball on the right, getting an early cross in as two defenders rushed towards him. Nicky Marker was there, but the cross had too much on it for him, and instead the ball came to Wayne Quinn, marauding down the left. Beating his man, Quinn steadied himself and took a shot with his right, only to see it go just over.

Deane then had his first chance. Paul McGrath's free kick came into the box from deep, Fjortoft flicked it on to set up the returning hero, but Perez had come out to close him down, and Deane couldn't get the shot on target.

Sunderland were unable to live with United, particularly Borbokis and Deane.

Deane was showing Unitedites what they had missed for four years, with 100 percent effort, skill and bravery. Winning the ball from the front, he now set up Borbokis who had made another raid forward. Sliding in to meet Deane's cross, though, he was unable to get any control on it and skewed it diagonally, Perez able to smother it.

Borbokis had shown his ability to attack, but now he showed the United crowd another weapon in his armoury, dead-ball delivery into the box. A free kick from the left, in line with the box, was delivered accurately and at just the right height and pace for Fjortoft, whose header flew just inside the post with Perez beaten. The only surprise about the goal was that it had taken 33 minutes to arrive, the Blades had been so dominant.

The Bramall Lane faithful had to wait just seven minutes for the second, though, and it was a beauty. This time, Fjortoft was the provider, playing a pass through the Sunderland defence for Borbokis. The Greek wing-back had made a run from deep and had timed it to perfection to meet the pass, beating the Sunderland offside trap. If his run had been good, his finish was great, into the far corner of Perez's goal from 12 yards.

It had certainly been one of the best opening 45 minutes of a Blades season. United had been irresistible and the faithful enjoyed the half-time sunshine buzzing about the football they had seen. On top of the fine attacking pace, the three centre-halves had kept Sunderland attacks to a minimum, working as a unit. McGrath, with knee problems that would force his retirement within weeks, had no pace, but his positional play was incredible. He was always in the right place at the right time without even needing to run, and his distribution showed why he had been one of the best in the business.

In the second half, with preserving the lead in mind, United dropped a little too deep, allowing Sunderland a few good chances. Dane Whitehouse cleared one off the line, Simon Tracey was forced to pull off a good save and Steve Agnew put one wide when he should have scored.

Spackman made a change, one striker for another, Petr Katchuoro replacing Fjortoft, and the move should have paid off, but the Belarusian forward missed two good chances. United were bossing the game again, and they looked comfortable. The big question now, and the thing that all of the Blades fans wanted, was whether Deane could score on his return.

It was a great team performance, but Borbokis and Deane were the standouts on the day, and the two combined to give Deane the chance the crowd were waiting for. Borbokis took on the defenders again, beating them and setting up Deane, whose effort cannoned off the underside of the bar and bounced clear. A Deane goal was not to be, but 2-0 had flattered Sunderland. On a sunny opening day, optimism around Bramall Lane was palpable, arguably more than ever before. Nigel Spackman's side had sent out a signal to the rest of the division that this was a team to be feared, especially with the two wing-backs and Fjortoft and Deane leading the attack. But, as we all know, supporting the Blades is never so simple.

v Coventry City 1-1 (AET)

(Penalties 3-1)
FA Cup Sixth Round Replay
17 March 1998
Bramall Lane
Attendance: 29,034

SHEFFIELD UNITED	COVENTRY CITY
Kelly	Ogrizovic
Short (Kachuoro, 64)	Telfer
Nilsen	Burrows
Borbokis	Nilsson
Sandford	Breen
Holdsworth	Boateng
Ford	Soltvedt (Strachan,96)
Marker (Dellas,72)	Whelan
Taylor	Dublin
Marcelo (Morris,85)	Huckerby
Quinn	Moldovan (Haworth,96)
Caretaker Manager: Steve Thompson	Manager: Gordon Strachan

Sheffield United fans of the last 50 years or so are used to seeing their favourite players sold to other clubs. Gone are the days such as when the club turned down a potential British record fee for Jimmy Hagan to move to Hillsborough.

In 1967, the club sold two of their stars, Alan Birchenall to Chelsea and Mick Jones to Leeds, within the space of two months. Later notables included Tony Currie and Brian Deane also going up the M1 to Leeds.

The arrival of Mike McDonald as chairman in 1995 had given Blades supporters hope that the days of the Blades being a selling club were over, and that the good times were on their way back to Bramall Lane as McDonald splashed the cash.

With the aim of a return to the Premier League under new manager Nigel Spackman in 1997/98, the team did not lose a league game until the end of October, and none at Bramall Lane. There were too many draws, though, which meant that they were always several points off the automatic promotion places as the season progressed.

There then followed several blows, which would have huge long-term implications to the club. Firstly, veteran defender Paul McGrath, who had been outstanding for the team, finally succumbed to a recurrent knee injury and was forced to retire from the game. Next, in a 0-0 at Vale Park, home-grown favourite Dane Whitehouse was the victim of a reckless challenge from Gareth Ainsworth which shattered his leg. Whitehouse never played again.

With no significant improvement in attendances, and looking likely to miss out on automatic promotion and so face the play-off lottery for a second season in a row, the club sought to recoup some losses (since McDonald had taken over, there had been a net transfer spend of £11.5m). An agreement was made to sell Fjortoft to Barnsley for £750,000.

Unexpectedly, Graham Souness, manager of Benfica, came in for Brian Deane. When Deane had rejoined United, there had been an agreement that he would be allowed to talk to a top club if they came in for him. This deal was honoured, and Deane left Bramall Lane for a second time. The club, though, still allowed the Fjortoft move to proceed. On 15 January, the news came that the club's two top scorers, with 20 league goals between them so far in the season, had moved on. Don Hutchison was also sold, for £1m to Everton. Nigel Spackman soon after resigned as manager. Demonstrations in the Cherry Street car park followed the next home game, McDonald and his 'evil henchman' Charles Green being the focus of much of the abuse. Kevin McCabe stepped in as football chairman to try to rescue the situation, with McDonald effectively cashing in his chips, although it would be another few years before he would sever ties completely with the club, and he remained the plc chairman until 1999.

McCabe promoted former player, and lifelong Blades supporter, Steve Thompson from the coaching staff, to manage the team for the remainder of the season. In spite of all of the turmoil, United had held on to a top six-position in the league, and they had also made progress in the FA Cup. Fjortoft's last goal for the club had been the winner in a replay at Bury in the third round, and Hutchison's last had been a penalty which was the only goal in the fourth-round replay at home to Ipswich. A win over Reading set up a quarter-final against Premier League Coventry at Highfield Road. The fates would have it that this would be Thompson's first game in charge of the team. Coventry were a strong team, sitting comfortably in mid-table and featuring former Manchester United striker Dion

Dublin, with 14 to his name already in this season. The Sky Blues were strong favourites to win, and the cup tie seemed to be following the script when United's defensive midfielder Nicky Marker brought down the Coventry manager's son, Gavin Strachan, to concede a penalty in the 32nd minute. Dublin scored from the spot to put Coventry ahead.

On the stroke of half-time, though, the Blades were level. Marcelo, the Brazilian striker signed from Alaves earlier in the season, skipped past the last defender and placed a shot that went in off the post. United had chances in the second half to win the game, but in the circumstances a draw, and a replay at Bramall Lane, was more than creditable. The following day the teams went into the draw for the semi-final. Kenny Dalglish's Newcastle awaited the winners. Between the two games, Reading were demolished 4-0 at Bramall Lane, so the team went into the replay with a level of confidence. The supporters rallied too, and the Coventry game drew the biggest crowd since the Sheffield derby of October 1993, delaying the kick-off by 15 minutes as the supporters crammed into the stadium.

Ten minutes in, though, United were behind. Kicking towards the Shoreham Street end, Coventry won a free kick 30 yards from goal. Boateng back-heeled the free kick into the path of Telfer, whose shot along the ground bounced twice before flying past a diving Alan Kelly and just inside his right post.

United tried to hit back almost immediately, Bobby Ford slicing wide from 25 yards after dispossessing Dublin.

They pressed again. Captain David Holdsworth found himself with a free header from a right-wing cross, but City keeper Ogrizovic defied his 40 years of age to pull off an acrobatic save over the bar. Vas Borbokis was brought down by Burrows for a free kick outside the area, the Greek wing-back took the kick himself, which flew inches wide. Coventry's lead survived to half-time, but only just.

The Premier League side started to assert themselves again in the second half, and a second goal would have almost certainly killed the game off. Boateng shot from 30 yards, forcing Kelly to pull off a good save, and Soldvedt could not capitalise on the rebound.

Their best chance fell to Moldovan with 15 minutes to go, when Telfer's cross found him free in the area, on pretty much the same spot that Holdsworth had headed from in the first half. Moldovan's connection was poor, and the ball went high and wide.

Time was running out for United, and a few supporters had already left the ground when Roger Nilsen's ball down the left to Lee Morris (son of former favourite, Colin), took a fortunate deflection for a Blades corner. There were less than two minutes remaining.

Borbokis put the corner into the near post, where it looped off a Coventry head back to Nilsen at the far side of the area. Nilsen headed the ball back across the goal, slightly behind Holdsworth, who swivelled, and hit the ball on the volley. It flew into the goal. As he and his team-mates ran to the corner flag to celebrate, those early leavers began to sprint back to their seats.

Into extra time, and Gareth Taylor had two chances to put United ahead. In the first half he couldn't quite make a connection with Ford's chip over the defence, while in the second he headed just wide from Nilsen's deep cross. Huckerby, though, probably should have scored a winner for Coventry but was denied by Kelly.

The whistle sounded to bring extra time to a close, and the game was to be decided by penalties. Holdsworth won the toss, and the Shoreham Street end of the ground was chosen for the shoot-out, five years and one day on from the night that Dave Bassett's Blades had beaten Blackburn on penalties at the other end of the stadium. Gareth Taylor stepped up first, hitting the ball straight down the middle, but Ogrizovic hardly moved, virtually falling on the ball to save it.

Dion Dublin, scorer of the penalty in the first game of the tie, was chosen for the first Coventry kick. He put it in the same place, to Kelly's left, but Kelly guessed correctly, and he too pulled off a save.

Kelly was the only player to still be at the club who had appeared in the Blackburn game, and he had saved the first penalty that night too.

Norwegian left-back Roger Nilsen, the other Bassett-era player still in the squad, now stepped up and took a convincing penalty, beating the keeper high to his left. Coventry also turned to their left-back, the ex-Liverpool player David Burrows. This time it went low to Kelly's right, but again he went the right way and saved it, deflecting it on to the opposite post and out of harm's way. United led the shoot-out.

Belarusian striker Petr Katchuoro was next up, but his shot blazed over the bar to give City the chance to level. Paul Telfer took a long run-up, and he put it in the same spot as Dublin had done with the first kick. Kelly went the right way again, and got his fingers to it, but the power behind the shot took it past him. Three penalties each, and the scores were level.

It was now Bobby Ford's turn. His was arguably the best kick of the night, confidently stepping up and stroking the ball into the top left-hand corner. The next taker for the Sky Blues was Simon Haworth, a recent buy from Cardiff. His kick, though, was a poor one, and Kelly was able to save. On St Patrick's Day, Irish international Kelly had saved three out of four penalties, and now the Blades were one kick away from a second FA Cup semi-final in five years. The responsibility was given to United youth product Wayne Quinn, who had been a revelation in this season. Striking the ball with his left, the ball flew into the top right-hand corner, and Bramall Lane erupted. Quinn stripped off his shirt and threw it into the Kop as supporters streamed on to the pitch.

Unitedites had been given a memorable night and a much-needed lift after a few traumatic months. They also had a semi-final at Old Trafford to look forward to. United gave a good account of themselves in the game, losing to a solitary Alan Shearer goal from a rebound after Kelly had saved. Newcastle's rivals, Sunderland, would prove United's undoing in the play-off semi-final a month later, despite United taking a 2-1 lead to the Stadium of Light, to bring a traumatic, but memorable, season to a close.

The season will be mainly remembered as the one where United sold Deane and Fjortoft on the same day, but the Coventry game helped to take the edge off the bad memory. The hero that night was certainly Alan Kelly, as he was on a number of occasions, not least the FA Cup semi-final at Wembley in 1993. The Blades have had some great goalkeepers over the years, but Kelly must rank as one of, if not actually, the best of the lot. Certainly, nobody who was there on the night against Coventry would have argued with that at the time.

v Leeds United 2-1

League Cup Third Round
6 November 2002
Bramall Lane
Attendance: 26,663

SHEFFIELD UNITED	LEEDS UNITED
Kenny	Robinson
Page	Mills
Jagielka	Lucic
Yates	Harte
Murphy	Woodgate (Duberry,63)
Montgomery (Ndlovu,57)	Barmby
Tonge	Bowyer
Brown	Kewell
McCall (Ten Heuvel,86)	Bakke (McPhail,71)
Asaba (Peschisolido,64)	Wilcox (Bridges,77)
Allison	Viduka
Manager: Neil Warnock	Manager: Terry Venables

After the big-spending seasons under the chairmanship of Mike McDonald ended in failure to return to the top flight, Unitedites returned to the familiarity of watching the club work under tight budgets and selling prize assets to cover debts.

Steve Bruce and Adrian Heath had both proven themselves unable to cope with the pressure of running a team on such a tight shoestring, so United turned to self-confessed Blade Neil Warnock in December 1999. Warnock, like Dave Bassett, had a track record of success with low budgets.

His first two seasons saw United play attritional, aggressive football. In both seasons, goals scored were below the divisional average, but goals conceded were too, and United finished in mid-table. The aggression came to a head against West Brom in March 2002, in the infamous 'Battle of Bramall Lane'. Three United players were dismissed, and the game was abandoned as two more left the field through injury with no remaining substitutions. The match made headlines around the world.

Warnock, cleared by the FA of any improper conduct regarding the game, rang the changes. George Santos and Patrick Suffo, two of the players sent off, never played for the club again, and a new squad was built around a young tranche of players, mainly Michael

Brown, Nick Montgomery, Michael Tonge and midfielder-defender Phil Jagielka. Veteran strikers Wayne Allison and Iffy Onuora were brought in, and the long-serving keeper Simon Tracey, the first to be sent off in the West Brom game, retired, to be replaced by Paddy Kenny. After three games without a win at the start of the 2002/03 season, the team then won seven in ten to put them into the top four places. In the League Cup, United had progressed to the third round with relatively straightforward wins over lower-league opponents York City and Wycombe Wanderers, and were rewarded with a home tie against Yorkshire rivals Leeds United.

Leeds and the Blades had plenty of history, even discounting the inter-city rivalry of being from Yorkshire's two largest cities. United had a record of selling their best players to the Whites, Mick Jones, Tony Currie, Gary Hamson, Keith Edwards and Brian Deane being amongst those making the trip, and the two teams had some memorable clashes over the years, including Leeds winning the league title at the Lane, courtesy of a Brian Gayle own goal, in 1991/92.

Leeds, under chairman Peter Ridsdale, had spent vast amounts of money on transfers and wages in a strategy (if you can call it that) that would, ultimately, be their undoing. Having spent over £100m on players, with no silverware or Champions League place to show for it, they had sacked manager David O'Leary and turned to former England boss Terry Venables. He had, though, shown little progress, and Leeds were mid-table by the time they travelled to Bramall Lane. Even before the game, Venables was getting press questions on his job security.

To put things into perspective, the Blades' entire starting XI for the match cost less than £1m to assemble, while the Leeds substitutes bench had cost ten times that amount. Leeds were firm favourites to progress in a competition that United had never had any real success in before.

A little out of character, Warnock's team showed an early lack of confidence in the game, and afforded Leeds too much respect and time on the ball. Kenny and his defence were kept busy. Kenny pulled off a save from a Mills effort, before Kewell under-hit a volley. It seemed only a matter of time before Leeds scored, but they needed some assistance, as Steve Yates, trying to shepherd out a Wilcox cross at the far post, mistimed his clearance, and put it past Kenny and into his own net after 24 minutes.

All United could muster was a 30-yard effort from veteran midfielder Stuart McCall, which, though it swerved in the air to cause some discomfort for goalkeeper Robinson to save, was going wide of the post. Leeds had a good chance to go two up with ten minutes left in the half, Kenny saving a bending shot from Viduka. Warnock felt that he could still win the game. 'If we could last the first five or ten minutes,' he said later, then the two attacking substitutions (Peschisolido and Ndlovu) 'would make a difference ... "Pesky" always gives a lift to the crowd.'

United certainly performed much better in the second half. Tonge's dribble drew a foul on the edge of the area, his bending free kick beat the wall and the keeper but went just wide of the right-hand post. Shortly afterwards, he set up Wayne Allison with a chance, but Robinson easily parried and smothered the shot.

Still the Blades came forward. Tonge was the driving force again, this time sliding a ball across to Michael Brown, but his shot from the penalty spot was weak and straight at the keeper. It looked as though it was not going to be Sheffield United's night. They were grateful, too, to Kenny for tipping wide a good shot from Viduka to keep them in the game.

The clock was ticking down. 90 minutes: injury time. The fourth official's board went up. Four minutes.

Tonge, wide on the right, beat his man and crossed. The ball ricocheted from a Leeds head.

Harte headed clear. Jagielka, 40 yards out, chested the ball back towards goal, took four steps, and let fly. 'The ball sat up perfectly,' the 20-year-old said after the game, 'and I just thought, "Why not?"'

The ball flew up and up and just inside of Robinson's right post, the back of the net bulging.

Three sides of the ground leapt to their feet, hugged, screamed, and danced with joy. So did Neil Warnock, never one to hide his emotions.

The Blades fans were only just taking their seats again as Peter Ndlovu played a ball through for Paul Peschisolido. Forced wide by a defender, 'Pesky' shrugged off a challenge to get the ball to the byline, and he cut inside so that he could play the ball with his left past another Leeds defender. Three Blades players were waiting in the area, including Ndlovu, who had continued running forward after the pass.

Now, in the same spot that Brown had scuffed the shot from earlier, Ndlovu found himself with time to shoot. He shot towards the centre of the goal. Robinson would probably have saved it, and dived in the right direction, but instead the ball struck Allison, played onside by Harte, on the back.

Harte and Allison now had a five-yard race for the loose ball, with the keeper on the ground. Harte narrowly beat him, but his touch only succeeded in touching the ball back to Ndlovu, who was left with a simple tap-in. From being a goal down with a minute to go, the Blades had won the game in injury time.

The whistle blew, and jubilant supporters streamed on to the pitch. Some, getting carried away, taunted the Leeds fans in the Upper Tier of the Bramall Lane end, and were pelted with seats torn from the stand by a section of the travelling supporters. The police intervened on horseback, moving the celebrating supporters back to the halfway line to celebrate, while the Leeds fans turned their anger away from the celebrating Unitedites and towards their own club, shouting for the resignations of Venables and Ridsdale.

In any other season, this would have been the greatest moment, but this wasn't just any ordinary season. United and Leeds would meet again in the FA Cup in March, the Blades would again emerge victorious, and this time it would cost Venables his job. The Blades' League Cup win over Leeds, and the Jagielka wondergoal, though, were just a taster of what was the come in an unforgettable season.

v Liverpool 2-1

League Cup Semi-Final, First Leg
8 January 2003
Bramall Lane
Attendance: 30,095

SHEFFIELD UNITED	LIVERPOOL
Kenny	Kirkland
Jagielka	Carragher
Quinn	Henchoz
Page	Traore
Murphy	Hyppia
Brown	Gerrard
Tonge	Diouf
McCall	Diao
Ndlovu	Murphy
Allison	Smicer (Heskey,57)
Asaba (Montgomery,50)	Mellor (Owen,70)
Manager: Neil Warnock	Manager: Gerard Houllier

The Sheffield United youth system has, like all clubs, produced some star players over the years, particularly in the 1950s and 1960s with the emergence of Alan Hodgkinson, Alan Woodward, Graham Shaw amongst others. In the late 1990s and early 21st century, the club made a significant investment in the system, hitting the goal of being granted 'Academy' status in December 2002. By this point, several players from the set-up were already first-team players.

Phil Jagielka had made his debut in the last match of the 1999/2000 season, aged 17, and had become a regular first-team player, with great versatility, playing at both full-back positions as well as a midfielder. After over 250 games for United, he would make a £4m move to Everton and eventually win 40 England caps.

Nick Montgomery, a defensive midfielder, had made his debut in October 2000, a week before his 19th birthday, and would make over 350 appearances for the Blades.

Attacking midfielder Michael Tonge made his debut at 18 towards the end of the 2000/01 season, and he too would pass the 200 appearances milestone for United.

Each of these three players would have 'their' matches in the memorable 2002/03 season. Jagielka scored his wonder goal against Leeds in the November, Montgomery would do a much-lauded marking job on Patrick Viera in a FA Cup semi-final later in the season, but the game against Liverpool in the first leg of the League Cup semi-final belonged to Michael Tonge.

Tonge had made a solid start to the season, scoring five goals in his first 12 games. In a 3-1 win over Millwall, he scored one and set up the other two goals, and he scored a fantastic winning goal against Grimsby. Although the goals dried up, he continued to cause problems for defences with his dribbles into the box winning free kicks and penalties for his team-mates, particularly Michael Brown, to convert. A number of top-flight clubs, Liverpool included, were linked with moves for Tonge, although these ultimately never transpired.

After the memorable injury-time turnaround against Leeds, United had been drawn against another top-flight team, Sunderland, in the next round. They deservedly won 2-0 with two goals in three second-half minutes from Shaun Murphy and Wayne Allison to put the club into the League Cup quarter-finals for only the second time in its history. A home draw against fellow First Division (as the second tier was then called) team Crystal Palace gave the club a great chance of reaching a first-ever semi-final. Super-sub Paul Peschisolido scored twice within four minutes of coming on in the 84th minute and the Blades won 3-1.

Any draw for the semi-final would have been a tough one, with Blackburn, Manchester United and Liverpool, all Premier League teams, in the hat with Sheffield United. It was to be Liverpool, who were three points off the top with a game in hand at the time of the cup game. All of the starting line-up were regular Premier League players, although Sheffield-born Neil Mellor was more used to being a substitute, and Michael Owen, named on the bench, was returning from injury.

United gave a first appearance of the season to Wayne Quinn, another home-grown talent who had been sold to Newcastle for £800,000 in 2001, but had now been brought back on a two-month loan deal. He was thrown straight into the team for the semi-final, in place of Jon Harley, whose loan spell from Fulham had just expired.

For the first time in almost a decade, Bramall Lane saw a crowd of over 30,000. The game kicked off and, as expected, United's Premier League opponents were the dominant team for the early exchanges. They should have taken the lead after 12 minutes. Diouf crossed from the left to Mellor at the near post who seemed certain to score, only to put it wide of Paddy Kenny's post, under pressure from two Blades defenders.

Liverpool continued to dominate, but the deadline was not broken until the 33rd minute. Danny Murphy's free kick on the right was flicked on by Hyppia. Neil Mellor, son of former Wednesday player Ian, slipped his marker, Robert Page, and headed home from close range at the far post. So far, and from a Liverpool perspective, going according to the script.

Shortly after half-time, manager Neil Warnock made a change, taking off forward Carl Asaba, who had been carrying an injury going into the game, and bringing on Nick Montgomery to change to a five-man midfield.

Almost immediately, United had a good chance to level the game. A poor clearance of a high ball from Mellor was met by the veteran Stuart McCall, a former Evertonian, on the half-volley 30 yards from goal, fizzing just wide of Kirkland's left post.

The game and the tie was then almost put beyond reach. Kenny, who had built up a reputation over the season as a great shot stopper, lived up to his billing when he brilliantly saved Diao's header from point-blank range.

United were also thankful that the referee was lenient with Michael Brown, when a lunge on the keeper was punished by a yellow card by referee Mike Dean when it could potentially have been deemed a straight red.

United endeavoured to keep the ball alive in attacking situations, a trademark of a Warnock team that would bring so many late goals. This almost resulted in a United goal as Wayne Allison found himself five yards out, but he could not get the ball under control enough to lob Kirkland, and it rebounded harmlessly off the roof of the net.

England star Michael Owen came off the bench, but it was time for one of United's two Michaels to write the headlines.

From a long kick from Kenny, Henchoz and Carragher failed to clear their lines. McCall's neat pass found Michael Tonge on the edge of the area. Looking up to see where the keeper was, Tonge brought the ball into his stride, let fly with his left foot, through the legs of Kirkland and into the net. Now 76 minutes had gone, and United were level.

The crowd behind them, United attacked again. Peter Ndlovu attacked down the right wing but his cross was put behind for a corner by Traore. Quinn's corner was swung into the edge of the six-yard box. Again, Henchoz's clearance was half-hearted, and fell to Tonge in the 'D' at the edge of the area. Tonge shaped to shoot but, showing good peripheral vision, spotted a challenge coming in from his right. Instead of shooting, he took a touch as the Liverpool player went to ground. Now with space and time, he powered the ball towards goal, this time with his right foot. Beating Kirkland through a forest of bodies, the ball took a bounce before hitting the back of the net. Tonge had scored two in six minutes, turning the tie on its head, and ran to the South Stand to celebrate as the crowd sang and danced to the tune of 'Tom Hark'.

Liverpool tried to scramble a late equaliser. Heskey was denied by a smart piece of defending, and Owen was flagged offside when attacking a rebound from a Kenny save. United held on for a famous victory.

Two weeks later the Blades and their supporters travelled to Anfield for the second leg, snaffling up tickets wherever they could in all sides of the ground. The slender lead from the first leg was, though, wiped out as early as the seventh minute, Diouf scoring from the edge of the box.

Just as in the first leg, United took the first half to settle into the game, but started to threaten Liverpool's goal in the second, Michael Brown's long-range effort from a free kick on the left forcing Kirkland to tip over early in the half, and they dominated for long spells.

The controversial moment of the game came with two minutes to go. Going up for a high ball with Wayne Allison, the Liverpool keeper fumbled, then lay on the ball outside of the area using his hands.

United supporters rightfully screamed 'off, off, off', but referee Alan Wiley only showed a yellow card, and the free kick from debutant Tommy Mooney went wide off the wall.

Liverpool won the game in extra time, the two England men Gerrard and Owen combining for the latter to score the winner.

Another exciting cup tie followed on the Saturday, a 4-3 thriller in the FA Cup against Ipswich to cap an extraordinary January where United won five games out of six in all competitions, and they had held Liverpool over 90 minutes in the other. They would go on to claim a fourth top-flight scalp with another win against Leeds, this time in the FA Cup quarter-final in March. This incredible season still had, arguably, the best game still to come too.

v Sheffield Wednesday 3-1

Football League First Division
17 January 2003
Bramall Lane
Attendance: 30,095

SHEFFIELD UNITED	SHEFFIELD WEDNESDAY
Kenny	Pressman
Murphy	Maddix
Quinn	Monk
Jagielka	Westwood
Page	Geary
Brown	Johnston
McCall (Montgomery,87)	Quinn
Tonge	Powell
Ndlovu	Robinson
Windass (Allison,73)	Di Piedi (Knight,73)
Kabba (Peschisolido,79)	Kuqi
Manager: Neil Warnock	Manager: Chris Turner

The big games came thick and fast in this season to remember. Sandwiched between the two legs of the League Cup Semi-final against Liverpool came the small matter of a Sheffield derby.

United were out for revenge. In September, in the game at Hillsborough, Wednesday had somehow managed to come away with a 2-0 win in one of the most one-sided derbies in memory. United had battered their neighbours, but goalkeeper Kevin Pressman, not for the first time, had performed heroics. United had fallen behind to a Lloyd Owusu goal on the hour mark, then were caught on the break as they pressed for a late equaliser.

It had been Wednesday's first win of the season and had lifted them out of the bottom three, but that was just one of two wins in their first 24 games, and manager Terry Yorath resigned. His replacement was their former goalkeeper Chris Turner, and there was some improvement with three wins in five from Boxing Day onwards, including a first away win in the game at Millmoor. They travelled to Bramall Lane for a Friday night kick-off in front of the Sky TV cameras, with the chance to complete a first league double since 1914 and to further continue their recovery.

The teams ran out to the theme to *Star Wars*, which was a preference of manager Neil Warnock's throughout his time at

Bramall Lane, but the crowd noise almost drowned out the music. There had been threats of violence before the game, and police leave in the city was cancelled as tensions simmered. A Blades supporter had been shot dead in a gangland shooting two weeks earlier, and Wednesday fans were searched to ensure there were no 'taunting' banners. A flare was fired by a United 'supporter' from the South Stand during the match, hitting a teenage Wednesday fan in the face. The game was attracting the wrong kind of headlines, but the football would ultimately win out.

Warnock had chosen to start veteran striker Dean Windass, who had returned to the Lane for a second loan spell after scoring three in four starts earlier in the season. He had also had a loan spell at Wednesday two years earlier, but he had failed to score for them.

The game started with the same intensity as the atmosphere. Heavy challenges flew in from both sides, not least Wednesday defender Garry Monk, who stopped a dangerous attack from Kabba.

A long-range effort from Kuqi stung the hands of keeper Paddy Kenny, then a jinking run into the area from Windass at the Shoreham Street end resulted in his effort being tipped on to the crossbar by Pressman. Peter Ndlovu's follow-up header was on target, but again the Wednesday keeper was able to get fingertips to it and put it over the bar.

Pressman again came toWednesday's rescue when a terrible defensive clearance by Geary had put the Owls in trouble. Windass put a superb ball across from the right, Kabba headed it towards goal but an outstretched hand by Pressman kept it out.

In the second minute of the second half, United must have felt a sense of déjà vu as, after Pressman's heroics had kept them out, Wednesday took the lead, just as they had done in the Hillsborough game. Alan Quinn somehow found his way through a mass of United shirts to find himself with just Kenny to beat, and he slotted the ball under his body and into the net in front of the United faithful.

United attacked, looking for an equaliser, and Michael Brown almost produced a moment of magic, beating three players as he dribbled into the box and powered a right-footed shot on target. Again, though, Pressman was there to deny a United goal, this time with a foot to the ball. Brown was enjoying his best-ever season with the Blades. He was a creative attacking midfielder with a powerful free kick, and he had been one of Warnock's first signings, from Manchester City in December 1999. Although Pressman had foiled his effort this time, his moment in this game would come.

After his quality play, it was a route-one approach that resulted in the United equaliser, just after the hour mark. Windass got his head to a long ball, Stuart McCall managed to keep it alive and put it into the box with his toe, and Kabba reacted faster than the Wednesday defenders to poke it into the goal, with the aid of a slight deflection.

After Kuqi scuffed a chance at the other end, there came one of the greatest goals in Sheffield derby history.

A free kick was played long into the Wednesday box from halfway by Phil Jagielka. Shaun Murphy, under pressure from two defenders, got his head to the ball but it wasn't a clean connection and floated to his right. Garry Monk got a strong head to the ball to clear it out of the penalty area but there, waiting and unmarked, was Brown.

He met the ball on the volley with a twist of the body, the execution was technically perfect, and, from 25 yards, the ball flew towards the goal.

Pressman had no chance, the shot bulging the net in his top-right corner, sending the Blades faithful into raptures. The goal had come in the 65th minute, just three minutes after the Blades had drawn level, and the game was turned on its head.

Then 13 minutes later, United put the game beyond doubt. Kabba made an unchallenged solo run down the right and into the box, taking the ball to the byline before putting the ball across, where Allison was waiting at the near post to knock it home. Allison's nickname, 'Chief', echoed around the ground. 'Chiiiieeeeeeeeeef!' Tonge could have added a fourth for United, but the game was won. Manager Warnock described it as 'probably the happiest of my life'.

Wednesday would eventually be relegated on Easter Monday, the same day that United clinched a play-off place. Wednesday's scorer Alan Quinn would cross the Sheffield divide in the summer of 2004, and he would become the first player to score for both teams in the Steel City derby.

Michael Brown finished as United's top scorer for the season, with a number of free kicks contributing to the total of 22, an impressive tally for a midfielder. Brown eventually felt that he needed to move to a bigger club though and, with his contract due to expire in the following May, he was sold to Spurs on New Year's Day 2004 for £400,000. He never really hit the heights again that he had hit in the 2002/03 season with the Blades, but his wonderful volley will be remembered, by Unitedites at least, as the greatest goal ever to grace a Sheffield derby.

v Nottingham Forest 4-3 (AET)

43

(Agg: 5-4)
Football League First Division Play-off Semi-Final,
Second Leg
15 May 2003
Bramall Lane
Attendance: 30,212

SHEFFIELD UNITED	NOTTINGHAM FOREST
Kenny	Ward
Curtis	Louis-Jean
Kozluk	Brennan
Jagielka	Scimeca
Page	Walker
Brown	Thompson
Rankine	Williams (Hjelde, 114)
Tonge	Reid
Asaba (Allison, 105)	Harewood (Lester, 61)
Ndlovu (Peschisolido, 105)	Huckerby
Windass (Kabba, 45)	Johnson
Manager: Neil Warnock	Manager: Paul Hart

The Blades have never had a season like 2002/03, and probably never will again. After two mid-table seasons under manager Neil Warnock, the team challenged for honours in all three major domestic competitions. Having gone out to a top-six Premier League club, Liverpool, by a single goal in the League Cup, they did the same in the FA Cup in a semi-final against Arsenal at Old Trafford. They were possibly also deserving of a draw, as a header from Paul Peschisolido that looked goalbound was denied by goalkeeper David Seaman pulling off what has been described since as one of the greatest saves of all time.

Canadian international striker Peschisolido, one of the game's journeymen with ten different English clubs on his CV by the time he retired, had joined United on loan from Fulham in the 2000/01 season and was hugely popular with the Blades following. A nuisance to defences with his tricky dribbling skills, he was a memorable feature of this 'triple assault' season, Warnock using him mainly as an impact substitute.

In the League Cup quarter-final against Crystal Palace, he had come off the bench in the 84th minute with the scores level and, by the 88th, had scored two goals to put the Blades through. In the FA Cup against Ipswich, he had scored an 89th-minute winner.

With all cup exploits over, United were able to concentrate on securing a place in the play-offs. They did so on Easter Monday with a win over already-promoted Leicester City, coming back from a goal behind to win 2-1 after a former Blades legend, Brian Deane, had given the Foxes a fourth-minute lead with his final-ever goal at Bramall Lane.

United finished the season in third place, which meant that their opponents in the play-offs would be sixth-placed Nottingham Forest, managed by former Wednesday player Paul Hart. With two of the division's top scorers, David Johnson (25 goals in the season) and Marlon Harewood (20 goals), in the team, Blades fans knew it would not be an easy task. Forest had beaten United 3-0 at the City Ground in November, although United had gained some revenge for this with a 1-0 win at Bramall Lane two days after the FA Cup semi-final against Arsenal.

In the first leg at the City Ground, tensions were high. Forest had the better of the play, and they deserved to go ahead when Reid found Johnson with a through-ball. One-on-one with Kenny, Johnson finished with style to put Forest ahead, ten minutes into the second half.

United responded well, though. Dean Windass, another veteran striker signed in the season, had a valid claim for a penalty turned down after former Wednesday defender Des Walker handled in the box. The ball was still live, though, and found its way to Michael Tonge at the edge of the box. Tonge played the ball back into the area for Michael Brown to run on to, Louis-Jean mistimed his challenge, Brown went down, and, this time, referee Clattenburg pointed to the spot. In front of the travelling Blades fans, Brown himself stepped up to take the penalty, putting it high to the keeper's left and into the net. Forest had defender Dawson sent off with seven minutes remaining, which ruled him out of the second leg, in spite of a Forest appeal against the suspension, and the game finished level.

And so to the second leg, and the largest crowd at Bramall Lane for 12 years.

United's line-up was unchanged from the first game, and they had the better of the first 20 minutes without being able to score.

Windass went close at the far post, and, just as he had in the first leg, had a penalty claim against Walker turned down after a challenge in the box. Another chance also fell to him, but he headed straight at Ward in the Forest goal.

The failure to turn chances into goals was punished when defender John Curtis, on loan from Blackburn, gifted possession to Johnson in the 30th minute. Johnson again finished superbly.

Both teams had good chances to score in the closing 15 minutes of the first half. Windass again had a good chance, this time deflected wide, while Harewood at the other end shot just wide with Kenny beaten.

At half-time, Warnock took off Windass, bringing on pacy striker Steve Kabba. Kabba had been on loan at Grimsby from Crystal Palace earlier in the season, and an outstanding performance for them at Bramall Lane had earned him an ovation from the Sheffield United fans. Warnock, too, was as impressed as the fans had been, and he paid Palace £250,000 to add Kabba to his stockpile of forwards. Kabba had scored on his United debut, and he had earned a place in Blades fans' hearts with the equalising goal in the derby against Wednesday, plus the winning goal against Leeds to book the FA Cup semi-final place.

As Kabba and United pushed for an equaliser against Forest, they were caught napping at the back. Mark Rankine was assigned to mark Huckerby, and while he complained to the referee about a decision, Huckerby found himself in acres of space as the ball was passed to him quickly. Huckerby fed Louis-Jean, attacking down the right from a full-back position. He had all the time in the world to cross and Reid, coming in at the far post, met it well to put Forest two goals up, in spite of Kenny's best efforts to stop it.

Two down after 59 minutes, and United fans began to feel that it was going to be three defeats in three semi-finals. This was no ordinary season, though, and still had twists and turns to play out.

Attacking from the kick-off, striker Carl Asaba was brought down by Walker on the edge of the area. After waiting what seemed like an eternity for the referee to move the Forest defenders back the required ten yards, Michael Tonge touched the ball to Brown, who shot from the edge of the area. The ball went through the wall, taking a deflection off Walker which wrong-footed Ward and into the goal. Seven minutes later Warnock's substitution paid off. A long ball from Kenny evaded everybody except Kabba, 15 yards from the Forest goal. With a goal reminiscent of Paul Gascoigne's famous Euro 96 strike against Scotland, Kabba flicked the ball up with his right and met it perfectly on the way back down, volleying it into the Forest goal. From 2-0 down in 59 minutes, the score was 2-2 after 67, and Kabba celebrated by blowing kisses to the South Stand.

With eight minutes remaining, Forest almost took the lead again, Phil Jagielka sliding across to take the ball from Johnson's left foot as he was about to shoot. The clock ran down, the referee blew his whistle, and the game went to extra time.

After an attritional first 15 minutes, Warnock again dug into his collection of strikers with two more substitutions up front, Paul Peschisolido and Wayne Allison replacing Peter Ndlovu and Carl Asaba.

Jagielka again provided a last-ditch tackle to stop Johnson at the beginning of the half, then, six minutes into the half, another substitution proved inspired.

As with Kabba's goal, it was a long kick from Kenny that caused the problems. Chesting the ball down on the edge of the area with his back to goal, Peschisolido turned, swerved to his left, then to his right, taking on and beating Louis-Jean twice before taking a shot. Keeper Ward was expecting a shot across his body, too late realising that the diminutive Canadian had aimed inside the near post. Ward was on his knees as the ball rolled past him into the goal.

As Bramall Lane erupted, Peschisolido ripped off his shirt, throwing it to one side as he screamed, 'Oh, my God! Oh, my God!' into the air.

Eight minutes remained, and after four minutes of them United came forward again, Kabba again causing problems. Catching Forest on the break, he found himself on the right with time and space to cross to Allison, who was clear at the far post. The ball never found its way to Allison, though, as Des Walker met the ball with his head and put it into his own goal. Mischeviously, United's PA announcer Gary Sinclair, caught up in the moment, announced, 'Scorer for the Blades, number four, Des Walker!', which got a huge cheer from the Blades support as they burst into a rendition of 'Tom Hark.'

United were two goals clear, and surely heading to the play-off final in Cardiff's Millennium Stadium. However, this game had one more slight twist left in the tale.

Forest attacked with Huckerby down the left. He took a speculative shot from a tight angle, which Kenny parried. Unfortunately for him, the ball rebounded off United captain Robert Page, and into the goal for 4-3.

With 30 seconds left on the clock, Forest came forward for one last attack. A long ball from Thompson found its way to Reid on the right, who crossed to the far post where Louis-Jean was waiting. He made a good connection, but Kenny was in the right place and smothered the ball. United held on for three minutes of injury time, and the referee blew the whistle for the end of one of the most remarkable games to ever take place at Bramall Lane.

'I've scored some good [goals] this season,' said Peschisolido after the game, 'but that was by far the best ... I just wish we wouldn't leave it until the end all the time.'

Warnock described the game as the best of his life. 'I never will be involved in another game as exciting as that. Anyone who came to that match will remember it for a long long time.'

After such an amazing game and season, the final proved to be an anti-climax as far as Blades fans were concerned. Wolves dominated, and were 3-0 ahead at half-time, former United striker Nathan Blake scoring the second. In the second half, United were awarded a penalty for handball. Michael Brown, who had scored six from six penalties in the season, saw the kick saved by keeper Murray, and a later shot from Tonge rebounded off the post. These two incidents summed up United's day and it was a long trip back to Sheffield for the supporters.

One of the most memorable seasons in their history had finished with nothing to show for it in terms of promotions or silverware, but the memories would last a long time, and the Forest game was, perhaps, the best of the lot.

v Hull City 3-2

Football League Championship
8 April 2006
Bramall Lane
Attendance: 26,324

SHEFFIELD UNITED	HULL CITY
Kenny	Myhill
Morgan	Thelwell
Kozluk	Cort
Unsworth	Dawson
Short	Delaney
Jagielka	Ellison
Armstrong	Fagan (Elliott,56)
Tonge	Andrews
Ifill (Kabba,87)	Green
Shipperley	Paynter (Duffy,56)
Webber	Parkin
Manager: Neil Warnock	Manager: Peter Taylor

For four seasons between 2002 and 2006, Neil Warnock's Blades flirted with the play-offs. After losing in the final in 2003, two draws in the last two games saw them miss out by two points the following season. The next season they challenged again, but they missed out after poor end-of-season form saw just two points taken from the last five games.

United had been 21st in the table when Warnock had taken over in late 1999, and he had crafted them into perennial play-off challengers, at the same time making a profit in the transfer market of around £2.5m over those six years.

No other club had been in the second tier for as long as the Blades at the time, and 2005/06 would mark their 12th consecutive season in the division.

Pre-season, Warnock wheeled and dealed again, breaking even in the transfer market despite spending £800,000 on midfielder Paul Ifill (the highest fee paid by the club for a player since 1997). This was balanced by the sale of Andy Gray to Sunderland, and Warnock used free transfers to bring in experienced players such as Neil Shipperley, Keith Gillespie and David Unsworth. All three were players with top-flight experience, taking gambles to join a Championship team with a hope of a quick return.

The moves paid off straight away, United winning 12 of their first 14 games of the season, and by New Year they were 11 points clear of third-placed Leeds.

Deciding to back Warnock, the board of directors loosened the purse strings, allowing him to make a 'big' signing (by Sheffield United standards) in the January window. Ade Akinbiyi joined for £1.75m from Burnley and scored after 12 minutes of his debut at Derby. He also scored in a 2-1 win at Hillsborough as United completed the 'double' against Wednesday.

This was, though, the only win in eight games and, with Leeds and Watford chasing, United needed to improve their form. After pulling off an impressive 3-0 win over Southampton, six games remained, and with a six-point advantage over the chasing pack, and an upcoming visit of Leeds to Bramall Lane, United could not afford to slip up.

Probably the last thing they needed, then, was a Yorkshire derby at Bramall Lane, against Hull. The Tigers had been promoted from the third tier the previous season, and they were safely in mid-table. Able to play without pressure, they had beaten Leeds the previous week, so United knew that this was not going to be easy.

As the game began on a rainy day at Bramall Lane, Hull delivered an early reminder that their opponents were in for a tough afternoon, as Irish international Keith Andrews pounced upon a loose ball by Michael Tonge, firing just wide of Paddy Kenny's right post from 35 yards.

The game flowed from end to end. United were awarded a free kick on the edge of the area after a foul on Ifill. David Unsworth's kick was on target, but was dealt with by Myhill in the Hull goal. Hull tried a long-range effort, Ellison firing from 35 yards and forcing Kenny to tip it wide of the post. The Blades then had a good chance to score the opening goal. Neil Shipperley picked up a loose ball in midfield and fed Ifill on the right. His cross was poorly dealt with by the Hull defence, the ball landing at the feet of Phil Jagielka who shot first time, but his shot bounced off the knees of the keeper. It could have very easily rolled over the line, but Myhill was able to fall on the ball and smother before it did. Danny Webber then took a leaf from Keith Andrews's book, going as close from 35 yards as the Irishman had done after cutting in from the left. The

Blades were starting to dominate the middle of the park now, and they made this count. Ifill, Kozluk and Tonge all combined on the right wing, enabling the latter to put a superb ball into the area for Neil Shipperley to guide home in the 36th minute of play.

Tails up, United pressed to double their advantage before half-time, Webber forcing Myhill to tip over with an effort from just inside the area.

The lead was eventually doubled seven minutes into the second half, Webber again involved. Sent clear down the left by a lovely ball from Chris Armstrong, he put in a pinpoint cross to find Paul Ifill running in to the near post. Ifill's partner had given birth a few days earlier, so his celebration was the obligatory baby-rocking dance with his team-mates.

United were two goals to the good, and Leeds were being held at home by Plymouth. 'Stand up, if you're going up,' was being sung by the United fans around Bramall Lane.

Any Blades fan knows that it can never be straightforward though. Sheffield United teams seem to love to put the fans through agony as much as possible. In the 65th minute, Thelwell played a ball in from the right, United's offside trap failed, Kozluk misjudged the pass and Elliott was found in yards of space at the far post. He had time to steady himself and picked his spot before rifling home.

Two minutes later, Hull could, and should, have had a penalty. Again the offside trap failed, and Duffy found himself one-on-one with Kenny, who was able to push the ball from Duffy's feet. It rolled free, and, as Kenny and Green both went for it, the Hull man went to ground, Kenny's hands around his foot. The referee, though, amazingly, did not spot the foul.

This respite for United was only brief. Playing with momentum, and now with the added impetus of feeling aggrieved, Hull attacked again. For a third time, the offside trap failed to work, Green collected the ball and squared it for Duffy to equalise, catching Kenny in the head with his knee as he scored. Just five minutes had passed between the two Hull goals.

Kenny was dazed, and he needed treatment. Warnock joked later, 'They said: "Paddy's dazed and doesn't know what's happening." I said: "Keep him on, he's normally like that."' Playing on, Kenny was then involved in a collision with one of his own team, Chris Morgan, when the tough-as-nails defender stepped in to clear a ball that the groggy keeper had been slow to clear.

Then it was United's turn to attack. Unsworth tried his luck from 30 yards and saw his effort touched on to the post by Myhill.

Into injury time, and, fresh off the bench, Steve Kabba latched on to a Shipperley pass, only to shoot straight at the Hull goalkeeper, the rebound put out for a corner by a Hull defender. Tonge floated the dead ball from the right corner over to the far post, where it was met by Chris Short.

Short headed it into the goalmouth. There, Webber met it on the turn, but the shot was straight at Myhill. The ball fell loose, and, reacting more quickly than anyone else, Unsworth blasted the ball into the back of the net from two yards.

The red-and-white sections of the crowd erupted. It was 93 minutes, and this crucial game had been won. Unsworth would describe it as the most important goal of his career, having described taking a drop down in division as a 'calculated risk.' United were now nine points clear of Leeds, with four games left to play. 'The games we have left are not easy,' said Unsworth, 'and I can't stress enough how vital it was that we won this one.'

The following weekend was Easter weekend. On Good Friday, in front of the Sky Sports cameras, United won at Cardiff by a single Danny Webber goal. Two good wins had put the pressure on Leeds and Watford who now had to win to stop United from gaining automatic promotion. Both teams came up short, drawing their games against Reading and Wolves respectively, and the Blades were back in the Premier League.

Unsworth, though, would move on, losing his place to new record signing Claude Davis early in the season and moving on a free transfer to Wigan in the January window.

It was a move which would come back to haunt United a year later.

v Arsenal 1-0

45

FA Premier League
30 December 2006
Bramall Lane
Attendance: 32,086

SHEFFIELD UNITED	ARSENAL
Kenny (Tonge,61)	Lehmann
Morgan	Senderos
Kozluk	Clichy
Jagielka	Touré
Armstrong	Hoyte (Fabregas,64)
Quinn, A.	Silva
Leigertwood (Davis,27)	Flamini
Gillespie	Baptista
Montgomery	Rosicky (Denilson,83)
Kazim-Richards	van Persie
Nade (Hulse,70)	Aliadière
Manager: Neil Warnock	Manager: Arsene Wenger

Few supporters were in any doubt that, having returned to the Premier League after 12 years away, the Blades would have to battle to stay there. Although they were denied an opening day victory against Liverpool by a controversial penalty award, it took seven games for United to secure their first win, against Middlesbrough with a 90th minute wonder goal from Phil Jagielka at Bramall Lane. The club had done well to hold on to Jagielka, who was attracting the attention of a number of more established top-flight teams, and it was credit to him that he stayed loyal to the club for another season.

Although the team picked up four more wins before Christmas, a home defeat on Boxing Day to fellow strugglers Manchester City left the club two just two points ahead of West Ham in 18th.

Four days later, Arsenal travelled to Sheffield. To put the gap between the two clubs into context, Arsenal had spent £6.8m on Czech midfielder Tomas Rosicky in the summer window. This was more than United's team on the day, including the five subs, had cost in total. In the first meeting of the two teams at the new Emirates Stadium in September, the Gunners had won 3-0. Most United fans, and probably Warnock and the players, would surely have been happy to take a point from the Bramall Lane return fixture.

Neil Warnock's team selection caused a bit of a surprise too. Perhaps with an eye on the 'six-pointer' trip to Middlesbrough two days later, and just two days after the defeat to City, he put top scorer Rob Hulse on the bench, replacing him with Christian Nade. Although he had made 12 appearances from the bench, Nade had started just one league game before this one, and his only goal had come in the League Cup against a League Two club, Bury. According to Nade, before the game Warnock had told him just to 'have fun, do what you can, and when you're tired let us know. He also told me that I could tear apart their defence, I just needed to believe it the same way he was believing it.'

Arsenal, though, were also determined to stamp their authority on the game, dominating the first ten minutes. Rosicky forced Paddy Kenny into a good save, Baptista was denied by a last-ditch tackle by Nick Montgomery and a downward header by Silva bounced over the bar.

At the other end, Rob Kozluk almost found Nade with a defence-splitting pass, then Alan Quinn wasted a good chance by shooting straight at Lehmann in the Arsenal goal.

On a pitch that had been cut up in the City game, free flowing football was difficult. This worked in United's favour as they nullified Arsenal's attack, the best chance in the rest of the first half coming from Aliadière but easily dealt with by Kenny.

Nade, meanwhile, was being marked tightly by Touré, trying not to allow him to turn, and Nade used this to his advantage with four minutes left of the first half when he received a pass from Quinn. Nade describes the action: 'I let the ball go between my legs because I knew he would try to keep my back to the goal. Then I knew I would get few steps in front of him [and that I] would win the race, and when I saw the keeper coming towards me I was already smiling in my head.'

Lehmann had rushed out of his area, and Nade fired the ball past him and into the open goal.

Half-time came, and United led. The pitch, which had so far worked in the Blades' favour, turned against them in the 60th minute. Kenny, taking a goal kick, caught his studs in the soft ground, and pulled his groin muscle. After the physio took a look at him, it was clear that his day was over.

Warnock had long had a strategy of not fielding a substitute keeper, figuring that the extra outfield option on the bench was worth the gamble of an injured goalkeeper. The multi-talented Phil Jagielka, who had played centre-half, full-back, and midfielder, was also called upon to stand in for Kenny should an injury arise. Jagielka had done this three times previously for the Blades, and his task now would be to keep out an Arsenal team which had scored more second-half goals than any other team in the Premier League, and who now threw on Cesc Fabregas to bolster the attack.

The Blades now defended en masse, and Arsenal struggled to find a way through. Captain Chris Morgan was letting nobody past, and it took until the 80th minute for the Gunners to create a meaningful opening. It fell to Robin van Persie, who found himself in a position to test Jagielka from close range, but the stand-in keeper pulled off a save worthy of any full-time keeper to tip the effort over the bar.

The clock ticked over 90 minutes, Warnock urging the crowd to get behind his team and their valiant rearguard effort. A long ball was punted into the box by the Gunners, and Claude Davis was forced into a last-ditch clearance for a corner. Arsenal sent everyone, including their own keeper, Jens Lehmann, into the box to test Jagielka and his defence one last time, but van Persie's corner failed to find a player. The referee blew time. Against all the odds, with unlikely heroes both up front and in goal, United had secured the victory, and moved five points clear of the relegation zone.

Warnock described it as 'Roy of the Rovers stuff'.

By 17 February, following a victory over Arsenal's rivals Spurs, the gap to the relegation places had increased to ten points. United were dealt a huge blow, though, in March, when Rob Hulse badly broke his leg in the game at Stamford Bridge when challenging goalkeeper Petr Cech.

Hulse had been integral to the team, both in terms of scoring goals, but also holding up the ball and general work rate. Following his injury, United would win just two more games, while West Ham would win seven of their last nine games, Carlos Tevez scoring six times.

Everything came down to the last game, a point against Wigan would send them down and keep United up, while a defeat would put the fate of the Blades in the hands of West Ham's result at Old Trafford. Former player David Unsworth converted a penalty to give Wigan the win while Tevez scored the only goal in the Hammers' win over an understrength Manchester United team. United were down, Warnock resigned, and a long saga of accusations and legal battles around the legality of the Tevez signing would result in United getting a £20m out-of-court settlement from the Londoners. West Ham, though, kept their Premier League status. Warnock's next job was at Crystal Palace, where he tried to sign Christian Nade. 'I had a very good relationship with Neil Warnock,' says Nade, 'he used to invite me to his place to talk and he told me that he could eventually get the Crystal Palace job in January and if he does he would like me to join him but I would need to play some first-team games. He advised me to go to Hearts and in January he will make an offer and bring me to Palace with him … but Hearts didn't let me go.' Nade would make a home for himself in the Scottish leagues, playing for nine different clubs in 11 years north of the border.

Jagielka would also leave United after the relegation, moving to Everton for £4m, and would go on to win 40 caps for England. His exploits in the Warnock years, in so many positions, earned him a deserved place amongst Blades 'legends'. Amongst Unitedites, memories of him are cracking goals against Leeds and Middlesbrough and the day he went in goal and kept a clean sheet against Arsenal.

v Aston Villa 2-1

46

FA Cup Third Round
4 January 2014
Villa Park, Birmingham
Attendance: 29,210

SHEFFIELD UNITED	ASTON VILLA
Long	Steer
Maguire	Clark
Hill	Luna
Collins	Lowton
McMahon	Bacuna
Flynn	Weimann
Doyle	Albrighton
Baxter (Coady,80)	Westwood
McGinn	Delph
Murphy (Kennedy,89)	Tonev (Helenius,60)
Porter (Miller,89)	Benteke
Manager: Nigel Clough	Manager: Paul Lambert

United had hoped for an instant return to the second tier following the disastrous relegation season of 2008/09, and they had turned to former Wednesday manager and player Danny Wilson.

It seemed a strange choice. Although Wilson had success in his first managerial job, taking Barnsley into the Premier League, his CV had been patchy since, and he had played no small part in Wednesday's relegation from the top flight, and had more recently been involved with relegations for both MK Dons and Swindon. His Wednesday connections did nothing for his stock with the majority of Blades fans.

The team, however, challenged for promotion throughout his first season, but went on to lose the play-off final to Huddersfield in a penalty shoot-out which came down to the goalkeepers and finished 11-10 to the Terriers. The following season also ended up in play-off failure, although Wilson did not see it out, being fired with five games remaining.

The board made another strange decision, gambling on a rookie manager, David Weir, to guide the team for the 2013/14 season. Weir was out of his depth, the team picked up just five points from the first ten games, and he was sacked. Nigel Clough had also been sacked just two weeks earlier after close to five years at his legendary father's former club Derby County, and United turned to him to turn their performance around. After losing eight in ten games under Weir, they lost just two in Clough's first ten, with the same squad of players.

Clough had come up the managerial ladder the hard way, spending over a decade at non-league Burton Albion, taking them up into the Conference and setting them up for a rise into the Football League, although he left for Derby four months before they actually achieved this dream. They had also held Manchester United to a 0-0 draw in the 2006 FA Cup.

Although the Blades weren't quite out of danger of relegation by New Year 2014, there was certainly a higher level of optimism amongst the supporters. As well as picking up in the league, United had progressed in the FA Cup, despite throwing away a 2-0 lead away at Colchester in the first round, Chris Porter scoring an 81st minute winner to put them through. Non-league Cambridge United provided little resistance in the next round, Jose Baxter putting the Blades ahead after just 12 minutes. The reward for a 2-0 win was an away draw against Premier League Aston Villa. At the end of September, Villa had won three from three in the Premier League, including victories away at Arsenal and at home to eventual champions Man City.

This early form, however, deserted them, and by the time the Blades rolled into town, they had won just three from 14. Although Villa manager Paul Lambert had made disparaging remarks about the competition in the run-up to the game, he sent out a strong team. Eight of the starters had played in the New Year's Day win against Sunderland, including star striker Christian Benteke, who was hoping to use a game against lower-league opposition to break an 11-game goal drought. United, meanwhile, were virtually unchanged from the team that had lost to Walsall on the same day. Few gave them a chance at Villa Park.

United supporters, though, relished the chance to have an away trip to a big stadium, after visiting the likes of the Bescot and Stevenage in recent trips. About 5,000 of them travelled to the Midlands, packing into local pubs before the game, and made a huge noise when the team took to the field. As this was the FA Cup, the away seating allocation was larger than in the Premier League, and the Blades were given both the upper tier of the North Stand and the first few blocks of the Doug Ellis stand.

While out-singing the home fans, the travelling Blades were rewarded by a confident start by the team. There was certainly no gulf in class in evidence in the early stages, and any Villa attacks were dealt with comfortably by the defence, forcing the Premier League side to try speculative shots from distance.

It did, though, take United 20 minutes to launch any kind of attack of their own, but they made the first one count. Jose Baxter found Jamie Murphy in space on the left and Murphy cut inside the box with the ball. His right-footed shot took a slight deflection off Clark and past Steer in the Villa goal, although arguably it would have beaten the keeper without the deflection. Cue wild celebrations from the Blades fans as Murphy performed a knee-slide in front of the Villa supporters.

United still kept the Premier League team at bay, although Benteke should probably have scored when heading Albrighton's deep cross into the ground and over for a goal kick. Benteke was valued at over £30m and would move to Liverpool at the end of the following season after scoring 42 goals in 89 games. 'We've got Chris Porter, Benteke is w***' came the ironic chant from the Blades in the stands following his miss.

This was Villa's only clear chance of the half.

Ryan Flynn had caused Villa problems down the right throughout the first half, and a few minutes into the second half came close to doubling the lead, finding himself with time and space to try a long-range effort from the corner of the box, forcing the keeper to tip wide. Villa then almost got lucky when Albrighton mishit a cross from the right which dipped towards goal, young goalkeeper George Long tipping it over. Benteke under-hit a shot straight at Long, while at the other end, a Blades academy product Matt Lowton, now at Villa, cleared as Flynn once again threatened.

With 15 minutes remaining, though, Villa found a way back into the game. A cross came in from deep which Harry Maguire couldn't head clear. The ball pinballed around the United box before falling to substitute Helenius, who rifled home. It would be Helenius's only goal in English football.

Not content with hanging on for a replay, though, the Blades attacked again, and once again Flynn was the threat. From the restart, he burst down the right and took a shot from 15 yards that flashed just wide of the opposite post.

It was a warning that Villa failed to heed. On 81 minutes, Ryan Flynn got his reward for the outstanding work on the right wing, cutting inside to somehow find space amongst three defenders to unleash a long-range effort with his left foot. It flew into the top corner, causing the travelling Unitedites to explode in celebration.

Flynn had been one of Danny Wilson's first signings as United manager. He was a Scottish right-sided midfielder who had come through the Liverpool youth ranks, joining United via Falkirk, where he scored the club's first-ever goal in European competition. Flynn had been a regular feature in his close-to three years at the Blades.

Flynn described the goal as the best moment of his football life. 'To score that goal in front of our own fans was just unbelievable. They came down in huge numbers and we heard them from start to finish. If anyone's in doubt of the magic [of the cup] then show them a video of that celebration, that's a special FA Cup moment, definitely.'

The final whistle came, and while Villa fans vented their anger at Lambert, the players celebrated in front of the jubilant away supporters. Some 51 places had separated the two teams at kick-off, but the Blades progressed to the fourth round. With promotion a virtual impossibility at this point, at least the cup had provided a day of joy. There would be more of these to come over the following months as the Blades under Clough built a reputation as cup giant-killers.

v Hull City 3-5

FA Cup Semi-Final
13 April 2014
Wembley Stadium, London
Attendance: 71,820

SHEFFIELD UNITED	HULL CITY
Howard	Harper
Harris (Hill,90)	Rosenior
Brayford	Figueroa (Fryatt,45)
Maguire	Chester
Collins	Davies
Coady	Elmohamady
Flynn	Meyler
Doyle	Huddlestone
Baxter (Davies,83)	Livermore
Scougall (Porter,83)	Boyd (Aluko,45)
Murphy	Sagbo (Quinn,64)
Manager: Nigel Clough	Manager: Steve Bruce

Nigel Clough had been appointed to the role of Blades manager in October 2013, with the team bottom of the third tier and staring into the abyss of a second relegation to the fourth tier. He was able to lift them off the bottom and, in January with the transfer window open, he was able to start bringing in his own players. Defenders John Brayford and Bob Harris came in on loan, while Scottish striker Stefan Scougall was signed for £400,000 from Livingstone.

In February, the team embarked on a winning streak of nine consecutive games in all competitions, pulling them well clear of danger, but the gap to the play-off places was too large to bridge.

Following the third-round FA Cup win at Villa Park, United were again drawn against Premier League opposition, this time at home to Fulham. Just as they had done in the Villa match, the Blades took the lead in the first half but, shortly after half-time, captain Michael Doyle was sent off and Fulham equalised. United were perhaps lucky to hang on, with Fulham hitting the crossbar, and the game went to a replay. At Craven Cottage, a tight game in heavy winds and rain was heading towards a penalty shoot-out when, with less than a minute of extra time to go, Shaun Miller headed home a corner to put the Blades through.

In the fifth round, Championship team Nottingham Forest came to the Lane, and there was more late drama. Forest took a first-half lead, but the Blades drew level midway through the second half. With the clock ticking down towards another away replay, former United player Greg Halford handballed in the box. Chris Porter's first task after coming on as substitute was to slot the penalty home. Moments later he tapped in a cross to put the Blades 3-1 up and to spark a pitch invasion by overexcited sections of the Blades fans.

In the quarter-final, a home draw against Championship strugglers Charlton was the most straightforward win since the second round, two goals in two second-half minutes booking a place in the Wembley semi-final. United's opponents for the semi-final were Premier League Hull City.

Hull had enjoyed large financial backing from chairman Assem Allam. Despite his investment, Allam was unpopular at the time with Hull fans as he was attempting to change the club name to Hull City Tigers. They had won promotion the previous season under former Blades and future Wednesday manager Steve Bruce, and, while not totally safe from relegation, were looking likely to finish mid-table.

Blades fans travelled to Wembley with low expectations, as the club's record in the big, neutral-venue games was abysmal. The last win in one had been in 1936 in an FA Cup semi-final against Fulham. Since then, in four FA Cup semi-final games and four play-off finals, the club had scored just one goal, Alan Cork's in the 1993 all-Sheffield semi-final at the old Wembley Stadium. This was only one of two goals scored by Sheffield United at Wembley in the club's history, the other being Fred Tunstall's 1925 FA Cup winner against Cardiff.

The Sheffield section of the all-Yorkshire crowd at Wembley hoped for a good performance and even, if they were lucky, a goal. This semi-final appearance was certainly more than anyone could have expected in the autumn, but now here they were at Wembley, with the club safely in mid-table and renewed optimism that Clough was the man to take them forward. The pubs around Wembley were packed and rang out with Blades songs. The supporters were there to enjoy the day out, regardless of result.

Sheffield United Greatest Games

With a larger traditional fanbase than the Tigers, United sold all of their tickets, while there were large, conspicuous patches of empty seats at the Hull end of the new Wembley, and a 4pm kick-off meant that the fans were well lubricated and in fine voice on a sunny April afternoon. The opening exchanges were cagey, with no real chances for either side, but any gulf in class was not immediately evident. Then, almost out of nowhere, came the moment that the Blades supporters had been waiting for for years. John Brayford took a short throw-in on the right, level with Hull's penalty area, and the ball was sent back down the wing in his direction. Brayford allowed the ball to bounce three times while he looked up to pick out a man, then hit the ball across into the six-yard box where it was knocked into the net by the onrushing Jose Baxter.

The team led in a neutral-venue big game for the first time in 78 years. While the Blades supporters went wild, Baxter, a Merseyside native, took off and kissed his black armband that all of the players were wearing to mark the 25th anniversary of the Hillsborough disaster.

Another scrappy 20 minutes followed while Unitedites sang their hearts out. Hull made a tactical switch, pushing Livermore further forward, and this paid off in the 42nd minute, as his through-ball split the United defence, allowing Sagbo to level the game.

Hull's celebrations lasted for just 94 seconds. Jamie Murphy, hugging the left touchline, worked his way past two Tigers defenders before putting the ball into the box from the byline. Scougall was there, and somehow he managed to find space between two defenders to put the ball into the net. Against all expectation, the team had scored twice and led the game. United fans headed into the concourse bars for a half-time party. Bruce's wing-back tactics had worked against him, both United goals coming from crosses, so he made a formation switch and a double substitution at half-time.

One of the subs, Fryatt, capitalised on some statuesque defending from a corner to bring Hull level within four minutes of the restart, and thought he had a second just two minutes later when finding himself clear and rounding the keeper, but the flag was (incorrectly) raised for offside.

This let-off for United was short lived, as, after three more minutes, Hull took the lead for the first time in the game. Huddlestone played a one-two with Meyler and finished with a touch of class with his left foot.

United were not going to lie down and let Hull steamroll them, though, and they attacked, Ryan Flynn beating the offside trap but being denied by an excellent challenge by Rosenior.

Sagbo, scorer of the first goal, picked up an injury, to be replaced by former Blade Stephen Quinn, who had joined Hull from United two years earlier. Just like the other substitute, Fryatt, had done, one of Quinn's first acts was to put the ball into the net with a free header from Livermore's cross to put Hull 4-2 up. Quinn, to his credit, didn't celebrate against the club that had developed him through their academy and whose two brothers had also been on the club's books in the past.

United heads didn't drop, they continued to push forward and created a couple of good chances, Scougall putting a shot over the bar and Flynn shooting at the keeper.

They were rewarded with a third goal on 90 minutes. Bob Harris found Flynn to the right of the box. Flynn flung himself at the ball, his flying header blocked by a defender, and it sat up perfectly for Jamie Murphy to volley home and give United hope.

Up went the fourth official's board. There were to be three minutes of added time, and United threw everything at Hull as a succession of shots were blocked from the edge of the area. From one block, the ball broke loose for Hull to counter, resulting in Meyler being one-on-one with keeper Mark Howard. Just as Huddlestone had done, he finished clinically to score Hull's fifth.

While Hull celebrated, the United faithful rose to their feet to applaud what had been an incredible effort against a team 42 places above them in the league structure.

While it may seem strange to include a defeat, with five goals conceded, in the list of greatest games, the context is everything.

The team scored more goals than in the nine previous neutral-venue big game appearances combined and had lead for the first time in almost 80 years in an FA Cup Semi-final (and then lead again). They capped off what had been an incredible cup run from the first round to, at half-time at least, dreaming of a first final since 1936.

There would be more cup exploits the following season, and another semi-final, this time in the League Cup. Ultimately Clough would fail in his primary goal, to lift United back to the Championship, and would be replaced at the end of that season.

For one sunny afternoon in April though, three goals against a Premier League team lifted Blades fans out of the gloom.

v Northampton Town 2-1

Football League One
8 April 2017
Sixfields Stadium, Northampton
Attendance: 7,425

SHEFFIELD UNITED	NORTHAMPTON TOWN
Moore	Smith
O'Connell	Moloney
Basham	Buchanan
Wright	Diamond
Freeman	Nyatanga
Lafferty	Anderson,P. (McWilliams,70)
Fleck	O'Toole
Coutts	Taylor
O'Shea (Hanson,53)	Williams (McDonald,81)
Carruthers (Sharp,45)	Richards
Clarke (Ebanks-Landell,82)	Smith (Revell,70)
Manager: Chris Wilder	Manager: Justin Edinburgh

It had been a long ten years since relegation from the Premier League. Since then, the Blades had lost a Championship play-off final, endured another relegation, failed in three League One play-offs, and had endured the Ched Evans saga while watching Wednesday overtake them for promotion. During this time the club had gone through nine different managers.

Entering their sixth successive season in the third tier, which also marked the club's longest-ever spell outside of the top two divisions, Kevin McCabe and the United board turned to former player and self-confessed Blades fan Chris Wilder to try to succeed where Danny Wilson, Nigel Clough and Nigel Adkins had failed before him.

Wilder had worked his way up the managerial ladder the hard way, coming through non-league football with Alfreton Town and Halifax. After leading Oxford United back into the Football League, he took over at Northampton. After rescuing the Cobblers from relegation to the National League in his first four months, he led them to the League Two title in his second full season.

The call of his boyhood club was too strong to resist. Within five days of the end of the title-winning season, he had moved to Bramall Lane. There followed a busy summer in the transfer market.

By the end of the August window, ten new players had been signed with 14 moving out. The players that had failed, and failed again, to get United out of the division were moved on as Wilder built a squad of his own making.

Initially, it looked like this turnover of players had been too much. Just one point was picked up in the first four games and, at home to former club Oxford in the fifth game, United went a goal behind in the 16th minute. At half-time, Wilder switched to a 3-5-2 formation, and the game was won 2-1.

Sticking with this formula, steadily evolving it into a style of play that would come to epitomise Wilder's Blades teams, United lost just three league games in the rest of the season. In fact, they lost to only two teams, as two of those defeats were against the same opponents, Walsall. By the time this Sheffield United team and their loyal support travelled to Northampton in April, they were 13 points clear of third-placed Fleetwood and six ahead of Bolton in second. A win at the Sixfields Stadium would see United celebrate promotion at the club Wilder had left less than a year before, and back in the second tier at long last.

Wilder had been replaced at Northampton by a fellow former full-back, Justin Edinburgh. The two managers had been on opposite sides as players in 1991 when United played Spurs. Now they stood in opposite dugouts. This was also United's first-ever trip to the Sixfields Stadium.

Northampton, barring freak results, were clear of relegation, although they needed two more wins to be mathematically certain.

With the Blades on the brink of promotion, demand for tickets was high, as the stadium only held just under 8,000. Many supporters gathered on the hill that overlooked the ground, from which they could see half of the pitch, but at least they would be able to soak in the pre-match atmosphere in the pubs, and, hopefully, the promotion party afterwards.

While Northampton had not played in the preceding midweek, United had a home win against bottom club Coventry, so Wilder made changes to bring fresher legs into the team, most significantly dropping captain Billy Sharp on to the bench and replacing him with ex-Wednesday striker Leon Clarke, who himself had come off the bench to break the deadlock in the Coventry game.

Sharp, a United academy product, was in his third spell at the club, and was top scorer with 26 goals at this point in the season.

The game kicked off, and Samir Carruthers, another midweek sub now given a start, came close to opening the scoring in the sixth minute. His dipping long-range effort rattled the crossbar as United, not surprisingly given the reward for winning, took the game to Northampton. Paul Coutts, who, along with Chris Basham, was one of only two survivors of Nigel Clough's signings in the line-up, also came close a few minutes later, shooting just over on the turn.

Northampton showed that they were not just there to make up numbers, though, and the second ten minutes of the game belonged to them. The Cobblers had three good chances to score, and one in particular should have been put away, but Marc Richards blasted it over the bar. Richards had been the top scorer in the title-winning season under Wilder, but his composure let him down this time.

The game became a scrappy affair, and the clock ticked down to 45 minutes. The home team had just about had the better of the half, and they were rewarded in injury time. United were caught on the break by a long ball upfield, which their defence failed to deal with. Cutting into the box from the right, Richards made no mistake this time, shooting from an acute angle and into the goal. Northampton were threatening to spoil United's party, or at least put it on ice for a week.

Wilder had resources to call upon, though. At half-time, Wilder brought on Sharp to replace Carruthers and strengthen the attack. After eight minutes of the half, he brought on another striker in James Hanson, switching to a three-man attack with Sharp and Clarke. Hanson had joined the club after a long spell at Bradford and had scored on his debut against Wimbledon, but this had been his only goal in Blades colours.

Wilder's changes were rewarded after 61 minutes. A lovely through-ball from Scottish midfielder John Fleck dissected four Northampton defenders, to put Clarke in a shooting position ten yards from goal. Clarke lifted the ball over the keeper and into the net with a sublime finish and ran to celebrate with a Blades fan who had run on to the pitch from behind the goal.

Eight minutes later United came close to taking the lead, again hitting the bar as Fleck met a corner with a close-range effort. The

Blades continued to press for the winner, Clarke and Coutts both having chances but could not find the back of the net.

Into the last ten minutes, and the news coming in from other games was good. Second-placed Bolton were losing by a goal at Scunthorpe and third-placed Fleetwood were 2-0 down away at Oldham, which meant that United would be promoted regardless of their own result. A draw in this game would still leave United seven points clear of Bolton with four games remaining in the race for the title, two of which were at Bramall Lane.

Perhaps with this in mind and deciding to hang on to the point, Wilder made his last substitution by bringing on-loan defender Ethan Ebanks-Landell on for striker Clarke. With two minutes of normal time remaining, though, the team put the icing on top of the promotion cake. A high ball down the right wing was flicked on by Hanson for Sharp to pick up in space at the byline. Four defenders were crowded in the box and only one United player, Fleck, was venturing forward, but Sharp was able to pick him out wonderfully. Fleck chested the ball down while still moving at pace, composed himself, and knocked it past the keeper and into the goal.

Cue a mini pitch invasion from the jubilant travelling support. Order was restored for a few minutes, until the referee blew for full time and the party really began. The entire Blades support swarmed on to the pitch, led by a fan who grabbed a corner flag and held it aloft as he ran, as though leading an army into battle. The support congregated in front of the main stand to cheer the players and playing staff.

The party continued in the Bramall Lane car park later that evening, as a crowd assembled to welcome the conquering heroes home, Wilder leading the fans in song as he stepped off the bus.

United's long wait was over, they were out of the third tier at long last. It was testament to the professionalism, spirit and attitude of Wilder's team that they didn't sit back. The remaining four games were all won, with United scoring three goals in each of them. The league title was mathematically secured on Easter Monday with a 3-0 win at home to play-off bound Bradford, and a final day 3-2 win over Chesterfield in front of 31,003 (the largest crowd at Bramall Lane since 2008) put United on 100 points for the season, the club's highest-ever points tally.

The title win also meant that United joined three others, Wolves, Preston and Burnley in a list of clubs to win all four divisions. The following month, Portsmouth also joined the list by winning the fourth tier.

The good times were back at Bramall Lane, and United had momentum to carry into the next season, back in the Championship at last.

v Sheffield Wednesday 4-2

49

Football League Championship
24 September 2017
Hillsborough
Attendance: 32,839

SHEFFIELD UNITED	SHEFFIELD WEDNESDAY
Blackman	Westwood
Baldock	Hunt
Stevens	van Aken
O'Connell	Lees
Basham	Jones (Joao,45)
Wright (Duffy,63)	Lee
Carter-Vickers	Bannan
Fleck	Reach
Coutts	Wallace (Butterfield,78)
Brooks (Lundstram,85)	Fletcher (Rhodes,68)
Clarke	Hooper
Manager: Chris Wilder	Manager: Carlos Carvalhal

'We gave you five years' sang Blades fans as they made their way to the first Sheffield derby in that space of time. The last one had gone Wednesday's way. United had joined them in the third tier and had been in second place, five points clear of the Owls in third with two games in hand, when the two teams met. Wednesday won 1-0 and picked up momentum, while United's top scorer, Ched Evans, was sent to prison for a sentence he later succesfully appealed. Wednesday overtook United in the promotion race, and the two teams had remained in their respective divisions since then.

While Chris Wilder had masterminded a magnificent 100-point League One title win in 2016/17, Wednesday had a promotion push of their own, reaching the play-offs for the second year in a row, but falling short again. With the resources of Thai tuna magnate Kraisorn Chansiri bankrolling the squad, including a £10m signing in striker Jordan Rhodes, they were amongst the favourites to succeed in their promotion bid at the third attempt. While Blades fans celebrated the title win, Wednesday supporters derided the achievement, describing League One as a 'pub league', conveniently forgetting where they had been just a few seasons earlier.

For Unitedites going into the season, the main thoughts were around survival. Wilder, though, was more positive, and set out to attack and surprise opposition, sending his team out on to the field with the motto 'be us'. The approach worked. Five of the first seven games back in the Championship were won, the two defeats coming in away games to teams that would eventually finish in the top six.

By the time the Sheffield derby renewed in September, just two points separated the teams in the table. A win for Wednesday would see them move above United and into the top six, and this is what their fans, the bookies and the pundits expected to happen, especially as United were missing their main goal threat, captain Billy Sharp, through injury. Wilder turned to former Wednesday player Leon Clarke to try to score against his former club. Joining Clarke in the United starting line-up at Hillsborough was David Brooks, a 20-year-old academy product who had made his first league start for the Blades the previous week, but who had impressed on a few occasions coming off the bench. The two players would have a huge impact on the game.

The pre-match build-up was soured by the decision to only give United supporters the upper tier of the Leppings Lane end and police cordons well away from the stadium aiming to prevent fan clashes meant that many didn't get into the ground until well after the game kicked off. This meant that they missed the first goal, as United came flying out of the traps and stunned Wednesday in just the third minute of the game.

Clarke, his early touches booed by the Owls fans, fed the ball to Brooks in the centre-circle. Brooks dribbled the ball down the left then cut inside, beating three defenders before eventually being bundled over at the edge of the 'D' of Wednesday's penalty area to win a free kick in front of the Hillsborough Kop.

The set-piece routine that followed was cleverly executed. Paul Coutts lined up to take it with Brooks standing next to the ball, but as he ran to hit it, Brooks back-heeled it into the path of John Fleck, who hit the ball sweetly, beating the wall and the keeper and into the net. United led, and the fans would get to relive the moment over and over again throughout the season, as Sky Sports included it in an advert for their 'EFL' programming.

Wednesday attacked Jones's shot from outside the area was blocked, then Adam Reach was unable to test Jamal Blackman, on a season-long loan from Chelsea, in the United goal when put through by Bannan, Reach putting the ball well wide of the post. From a United corner, the ball fell to Fleck on the edge of the area, but he was easily blocked, and the ball fell to Wednesday's Wallace. He tried to launch a quick counter-attack with a high ball towards Lee but United left-back Enda Stevens saw the danger, and he launched the ball clear. The high clearance bounced in the middle of a circle of six blue shirts, but the ball evaded them all. Leon Clarke, the only Blades player in advance of the halfway line, gambled on the Wednesday players not clearing the ball, and now latched on to it.

One-on-one with keeper Westwood, with van Aken bearing down on him, he finished well. Just 15 minutes gone, and the Blades were 2-0 up.

He came close to scoring again ten minutes later, too, putting just wide, and Chris Basham also had a good chance, but mishit his chance over the bar. At the other end, the Blades defence kept Wednesday's forwards at bay, and they didn't have another shot on goal until the 45th minute when Hunt pounced on a loose headed clearance to shoot from 25 yards. His shot looked goalbound, but centre-back Jake Wright was brilliantly able to get his head to it and put it over the bar for a corner.

With seconds ticking down to the end of the half Wednesday launched one last attack, and this time it was a successful one. Hunt, knowing that time was short, launched a long ball from right-back and the ball found its way to Wallace on the right wing, who hooked the ball into the box. Striker Gary Hooper reacted faster than the United defenders around him, and put the ball past Blackman. At half-time, Wednesday manager Carvalhal made a tactical switch, bringing a more attacking midfielder on in Lucas Joao for Jones, and there was an immediate improvement in Wednesday's attacking play, although they were still being limited to long-range efforts. Both Lee and Wallace had theirs blocked and then Reach almost got lucky with a deflected one.

A defence-splitting ball from Reach almost put Hooper through, but his touch let him down and Blackman was able to grasp the ball.

Then came a moment of magic from David Brooks for United. Following a spell of head-tennis from a Wednesday corner, Chris

Basham was able to find the young midfielder on the left touchline with the ball, although Brooks was still under close pressure from Hunt. As he turned, he nutmegged Hunt and sprinted away from him with the ball, finding Clarke in space with a lovely cross. Clarke controlled the ball well, but his effort didn't match the quality that had come before and the ball sailed over the bar, to the delight of the jeering Wednesday fans.

Brooks's break showed that Wednesday were vulnerable on the flanks, so Wilder made a tactical switch, bringing Mark Duffy on for defender Wright and switching from three to four at the back. United fans must have feared that Clarke's miss would be a costly one, though, when Wednesday equalised in the 65th minute. Tricky play by Lee in the middle of the pitch resulted in Reach being able to take the ball down the left wing. His early cross should have easily been cut out by Cameron Carter-Vickers, but the Spurs loanee slipped at the vital moment. The ball fell to the substitute, Joao, who had time to compose himself and rifle home.

The Wednesday fans were jubilant. They had come back from two goals down to level the game and 30,000 of them were on their feet, jumping up and down singing, 'If you don't ****ing bounce then you're a Blade'. The stadium was rocking.

But then United came forward. Mark Duffy played a one-two with Clarke to work his way into the right-hand side of the Wednesday area, and the bouncing Wednesday fans froze in fear of what was to come.

Duffy twisted left, then right, to beat van Aken, and shot from an acute angle at the near post. The ball flew past Westwood and into the net. United were ahead again, just two minutes after the scores had been levelled.

The goal, and its effect on the Wednesday supporters, would go viral on the internet, and instantly become part of Blades folklore. Duffy, the 'Bounce Killer', had come off the bench and silenced the Hillsborough faithful. Blades fans and captain Billy Sharp later tweeted, 'Got woken up at 2 minutes to 4 last night by the kids bouncing on the bed, Mark Duffy came in and put them back to sleep.' The game wasn't over yet though. Bannan's long-range effort went just wide, then Brooks had a chance after a great run into the box from the left, forcing Westwood to parry the ball over.

United sealed the victory in the 77th minute. Brooks fed the ball forward for Clarke to muscle his way between two defenders and poke the ball past the keeper.

Given the game they both had, it was fitting that Brooks and Clarke were the combination that got the goal. Clarke had scored two and played Duffy in for another, while Brooks had caused problems for Wednesday all day, winning the free kick that led to the first goal and setting up Clarke for the fourth.

Wednesday had a couple of chances for a consolation goal, but the game finished 4-2. In a season where United had been expected just to survive, and Wednesday to challenge, United now went into the top four, and the following month would go top after a win at Leeds, while Wednesday spent most of the rest of the season in the lower half of the table. Manager Carvalhal was fired, and his replacement's debut was the return Steel City derby game at Bramall Lane, when they were delighted to come away with a 0-0 draw.

A bad injury to Coutts away at Burton would start a poor run of form for United that would see them drop out of the play-off picture by the season's end, but it had been a memorable return to the second tier, and would be a precursor for a bigger campaign the following season. The win at Hillsborough would even have its own song from the Blades supporters, to the tune of 'Oh What a Night' by the Four Seasons.

'Oh, what a night.
Late September 2017,
Smashed the Piggies
With our Pub League Team.
What a Feeling.
What a night'

v Ipswich Town 2-0

EFL Championship
27 April 2019
Bramall Lane
Attendance: 30,140

SHEFFIELD UNITED	IPSWICH TOWN
Henderson	Gerken
Baldock	Chambers
Stevens	Nsiala
O'Connell	Kenlock
Egan	Bree
Basham	Skuse
Fleck	Bishop
Norwood	Downes
Duffy (Lundstram,85)	Judge
Hogan (Sharp,63)	Jackson (Dozzell,68)
McGoldrick (Madine,75)	Keane (Chalobah,8)
Manager: Chris Wilder	Manager: Paul Lambert

I began writing this book at the beginning of 2018, a few months after the 4-2 win over Wednesday, which I had planned to be the last game included. As I began, United had just come off the back of a run of one win in ten matches, following the bad injury to Paul Coutts away at Burton, and were on a slide which would see them finish in tenth place, although they were still in with a slight chance of making the play-offs with two games to go. Still, a very respectable first season back in the Championship.

In the summer that followed, manager Chris Wilder set out to strengthen the squad, using some of the funds made available through the sale of David Brooks, to Premier League Bournemouth, to sign central defender John Egan from Brentford for a club-record £4.1m. He also turned to the loan market, bringing in England under-21 keeper Dean Henderson from Manchester United, midfielder Oliver Norwood from Brighton (who had been in Championship promotion-winning teams for the previous two seasons with Brighton, then on loan at Fulham), and bringing in two free transfers in David McGoldrick and Martin Cranie.

Each of these players were signed with a specific role in mind, and each worked perfectly, improving Wilder and his assistant manager Alan Knill's 'overlapping centre-back' 3-5-2 system so much so that, despite the defenders venturing forward, the team had the joint-best defensive record in the division by the end of the season. Meanwhile, up front, McGoldrick proved an inspired improvement on Leon Clarke, who himself had done a good job for the Blades. McGoldrick and club captain Billy Sharp scored 38 goals between them in the season. United were in the top four for the majority of the season, occasionally topping the league but challenged by Norwich, West Brom and, of all clubs, Yorkshire rivals Leeds. As 2019 arrived, Wilder made three more loan signings to add more firepower up front. Young Irish international Scott Hogan came in from Villa, midfielder Kieran Dowell came from Everton, but the third was a little controversial.

Gary Madine had played for Wednesday in the past and had been caught on camera the worse for wear calling Sharp a 'little fat pig'. Sharp made it clear that he had no issue with the signing, laughing it off by saying 'I don't think he said anything that people don't already know... I think everybody knows I'm fat!'

By March, I had finished the final draft of this book, and sent it into Pitch Publishing. Two days earlier, the Blades had travelled to Elland Road for a crunch meeting with Leeds.

United had recently won impressively at the Hawthorns to effectively knock West Brom out of the race for automatic promotion and, prior to heading up the M1, had kept six successive clean sheets.

At Leeds, they pulled off a perfect smash-and-grab, Chris Basham scoring with the only shot on target in the entire game despite the Blades having less than 30 per cent of the possession.

The win put United a point ahead of Leeds, with eight games left to play. With United guaranteed a play-off place, Pitch and I agreed that we would not send the book to the printers just yet. Things were looking good.

Being a football fan, and therefore naturally superstitious, I feared that this decision might have put the curse on the team, as United won just one of the next four games, the fourth being a 1-1 draw at home to Millwall, with the Lions' equaliser coming in the fifth minute of injury time.

Blades fans were put in the uncomfortable position of wanting an Owls victory later that evening, but Leeds tore Wednesday apart at Elland Road to set up a three-point lead over the Blades.

With many of the games now selected for live TV coverage, the remaining fixtures all meant that United played before Leeds except for the very last game. The first set of fixtures came on Good Friday, United easily beating Forest 2-0, but Leeds were expected to brush relegation-threatened Wigan aside with no problems in the late kick-off.

Leeds choked, despite Wigan playing with ten men for 76 minutes. Leeds missed a penalty, and were caught on the break twice, Wigan scoring (just like United had done against Leeds) with their only shots on target.

Further Easter joy followed on the Monday. United travelled to Hull, who had not been beaten at home since the November. McGoldrick was in superb form, scoring twice in 22 minutes, the second an absolute stunner. The Blades, backed by a huge away following, were 3-0 up by half-time and this is how it stayed. The pressure was really on Leeds now, and again, proved too much for them as they were outplayed by a good Brentford team at Griffin Park. They lost 2-0.

Three points ahead of Leeds now, with two games remaining and a much superior goal difference, United knew that a win at home to Ipswich would all-but clinch promotion.

Ipswich were already relegated, having won just seven games all season, so the bookies made United clear favourites. Blades fans, though, have seen it all before, and there were many of us still nervous about making it over the line, especially as Leeds were due to play Ipswich in their last game which, so most people thought, would be an easy three points for them.

30,140 packed into Bramall Lane to cheer United over the line, and they were in fine voice throughout.

After an early delay for treatment to Ipswich striker Keane resulted in him being substituted United, kicking towards the Bramall Lane end in bright sunshine, began to exert pressure on the visitors, which resulted in an Ipswich defender giving the ball away cheaply to John Fleck. The ball broke to Scott Hogan, who played a one-two with Fleck into the area. Hogan, though, sliced the chance wide.

Although United were dominating play, chances were few and far between for the first quarter of the game, and there was always the danger that Ipswich would catch them on the break. This almost happened in the 23rd minute, as loose play in midfield allowed Bishop to slalom his way into the box and get a shot away, but Chris Basham stretched out his leg to block the shot.

Within moments, United were on the attack again. A low cross from Baldock was cleared but the Blades picked it up in midfield, building patiently on the left, allowing time for O'Connell to get forward. He took the ball to the byline and sent a cross into the six-yard box. There to meet it was Hogan, and this time he made no mistake, touching the ball into the net to send Bramall Lane wild.

The goal was a perfect example of the Wilder-Knill style of play, the overlapping centre-back causing problems for defenders unsure of who to mark, which either bought the midfielders and wing-backs more space, or saw the central defenders cross themselves, as O'Connell had done here.

If the noise levels had been high before, they were even higher now, and the stadium reverberated with chants of 'Chrissy Wilder, he's one of our own.'

The team continued to dominate. Norwood shot from distance from a well-worked corner routine, but his on-target shot was blocked. Within two minutes, McGoldrick played a defence-splitting ball to find Baldock in the area, but his eventual shot was charged down.

Norwood put another chance wide as Ipswich aimed to hold on to half-time to regroup. They could, and probably should, have been down to ten men by then, Alan Judge guilty of a studs-up challenge on his former Brentford team-mate O'Connell but getting away with a yellow card despite Wilder's protestations from the sideline.

The second half began with more United dominance. After they won an early free kick on the left, Norwood shot directly from an acute angle, the effort cannoning back off the post. Shortly afterwards, he saw another long-range effort blocked.

Norwood was involved again in the next chance, his pinpoint cross to the far post finding David McGoldrick, who headed just wide.

With so many chances going begging, there was always the chance that Ipswich could sneak an equaliser. It would have been totally against the run of play, but football can be a cruel game. A second United goal would completely kill off a poor Ipswich team, so Wilder brought on captain and top-scorer Billy Sharp to try to put the game, and the promotion race, to bed.

It was defenders, though, that would feature in the next two attacks. John Egan headed a corner over from close range but the next corner, just a minute later, saw Jack O'Connell outjump everyone else at the far post to head the ball into the net. With 71 minutes gone, United had the crucial second, and were almost over the line.

The rest of the game passed by without much incident. United knew the job was done and the final whistle saw celebrations on the pitch and around the stadium, which carried on to London Road well after the stadium had emptied, closing the road down for an impromptu, beer-fuelled carnival.

There was still the slimmest chance of Leeds catching United, but they had to win their next two games and overturn a huge goal difference. They played an in-form Villa the day after the Ipswich game, which turned out to be a strange affair. Leeds scored an 'unsportsmanlike' goal with a Villa player down injured and their manager, Bielsa, allowed his opponents to walk in an equaliser unchallenged. They were the only two goals of the game, which guaranteed United's promotion.

While the events at Elland Road unfolded, the United team and staff were enjoying their Player of the Year awards dinner, and a huge celebration ensued. 'It's one of the greatest days of my life, 100%,' said Wilder. 'To see it over the line today, surrounded by my players and my family, to see us back in the Premier League is truly incredible. What a day to be a Blade. Next season will be a fabulous experience for everyone involved.'

Wilder had now won promotion from every division of the Football League, and the National League too, while captain Sharp had completed a lifelong ambition. 'To get one promotion with my boyhood club is something, but to then do it twice and get to the Premier League is incredible and I'm going to enjoy every bit of it now.' The team had done it in style, playing entertaining football with a squad of all British/Irish players and a manager and a captain who were both 'one of us' – there had been promotions to the top flight before, but this one would take some beating.

Bibliography

Barnard, R., *The Jimmy Hagan Story* (The History Press, 2007)

Bassett, D., *Settling the Score* (John Blake, 2002)

Clarebrough, D., *Sheffield United – The First 100 Years* (SUFC, 1989)

Clarebrough, D. & Kirkham, A., *Sheffield United F.C. 1889–1999 A Complete Record* (SUFC, 1999)

Clarebrough, D. & Kirkham, A., *Sheffield United F.C. Who's Who* (The Hallamshire Press, 2008)

Farnsworth, K., *Blades & Owls* (Breedon Books, 1995)

Farnsworth, K., *Sheffield Football, A History – Volumes I and II* (The Hallamshire Press, 1995)

Hodgkinson, A., *Between the Sticks* (HarperCollins, 2014)

Huntley, E., *The Matador: The Life and Career of Tony Currie* (Pitch Publishing 2015)

Needham, E., *Association Football* (1901. Reprint by Soccer Books, 2003)

Phythian, G., *Colossus: The True Story of William Foulke* (Tempus, 2005)

Waterman, G., *Ooh-Aah, The Bob Booker Story* (Bennion Kearny, 2017)

The Times and the *Sunday Times* archive

The Mail Online, January 2014 https://www.dailymail.co.uk

Backpass magazine, issue 59

English National Football Archive, www.enfa.co.uk

England Football Online, www.englandfootballonline.comNews papers at the British Newspaper Archive:

The *Daily Herald* 1958

The *Daily Mirror* 1958

The *Guardian* 2006

The *Independent* 2006

Sheffield Daily Telegraph 1891–1950

Sheffield Independent 1891–1938

The Star, the *Star Green 'Un/Sheffield Evening Telegraph* 1925–98

The Sportsman 1892, 1902

The *Sporting Life* 1899, 1902

The *Sunday Mirror* 1915